THE GENTLE MESSENGER

An Authentic Psychic's Story

REBECCA BARTLETT

iUniverse LLC
Bloomington

THE GENTLE MESSENGER
AN AUTHENTIC PSYCHIC'S STORY

iUniverse books may be ordered through booksellers or by contacting:

iUniverse LLC
1663 Liberty Drive
Bloomington, IN 47403
www.iuniverse.com
1-800-Authors (1-800-288-4677)

Because of the dynamic nature of the Internet, any web addresses or links contained in this book may have changed since publication and may no longer be valid. The views expressed in this work are solely those of the author and do not necessarily reflect the views of the publisher, and the publisher hereby disclaims any responsibility for them.

Any people depicted in stock imagery provided by Thinkstock are models, and such images are being used for illustrative purposes only.

Certain stock imagery © Thinkstock.

ISBN: 978-1-4759-8667-9 (sc)
ISBN: 978-1-4759-8668-6 (e)

Printed in the United States of America

iUniverse rev. date: 11/23/2013

❈ Author's Note

This is a book about the journey of a psychic. This book explores the realization, development and use of my abilities. There is not one fabrication. The names of those I have worked with confidentially have been changed to protect their identity.

Acknowledgements

I am tremendously grateful to Michele Pollock for voluntarily editing my original manuscript.

❋ Dedication

I owe a debt of gratitude and appreciation to each client who has had the faith to come in to see me to gain insight, guidance, knowledge and comfort.

Table of Contents

❧ Glossary
of My Psychic Experience

apocalyptic	An Apocalypse is anything viewed as a Revelation.
aura	An invisible emanation produced by and surrounding a person or object, discernible by individuals of supernormal sensibility.
automatic writing	Writing from a subconscious or spiritual source without awareness of the content.
clairvoyance	Knowledge of information not necessarily known to any other person, not obtained by ordinary channels of perceiving or reasoning – thus a form of extrasensory perception (ESP).
medium	A person "in-between," an intermediary between the deceased and the living
nimbus	A surrounding aura or atmosphere.
inspiration	Divine guidance exerted directly upon the mind and soul of man.

pre-cognitive	Knowledge of things before they exist or happen; foreknowledge; foresight.
premonition	An intuition of a future, usually unwelcome, occurrence; foreboding; an early warning of a future event; forewarning.
psi	Scientific acronym for unusual mental events.
psi-intel	A term applied to intelligence collecting, in this case gathered through formal ESP measures.
psychometry	The ability to divine facts concerning an object or a person associated with it, by contact with or proximity to an object belonging to the person. Derived from the Greek, meaning "measuring the soul of things."
remote viewing	The practice of seeking impressions about a distant or unseen target using paranormal means, in particular, extra-sensory perception (ESP) or sensing with the mind.
telepathy	From the Greek τηλε, (tele) meaning "distant" and πάθη, (pathe) meaning "affliction, experience." The induction of mental states from one mind to another.
visitation	A dream conveying a message "in person" to the dreamer.

❈ Introduction

In my past I have walked up to people from all levels of importance, imploring them to listen to the words I tell them. Very few would pay any attention at all. In most cases I was not given the time of day. Imagine that—I wasn't looking for compensation; I just wanted to help them with what may be life-saving information.

No one knew who I was—who I had been behind the scenes as over the years historic events took place that I had predicted. I had the gift, as they say. But it was all orchestrated privately. No witnesses. No fame. Just an uncanny knowledge and need to tell. Though I could save lives in real time I had no voice and no encouragement...just blank stares and cross-eyed looks. And here I was wasting my gifts at a menial job five years after psychically tracking down the footsteps of one of Americas top-ten most wanted terrorist fugitives.

I wish people would not ignore the messages that could mean so much to them.

There is no price you could pay for a forewarning, but there is a heavy toll of ignoring someone like me in time. Please don't deny what is divine; don't only expect to see fraud—look deeper. I would like to ask that you be patient and understanding. Every utterance, every account, every feeling I discuss in these pages is the complete truth.

🏵 1 Apocalyptic

*Every great dream begins with a dreamer.
Always remember, you have within you the
strength, the patience, and the passion to
reach for the stars to change the world.*

—Harriet Tubman

Have you ever awoken with a sense of uneasiness that something
was going to go wrong that day? That is essentially the story of
my life. I can feel the future. The first prophecy I remember?
Knowing the last name of my future fiancé. It happened while I
was walking on my way to kindergarten.

I appreciated an unmistakable sense of something very pure
and powerful giving me that insight. What some might relate
to as a "gut" sensation was for me very matter-of-factly an all-
over knowingness. There was no questioning, just the acceptance
of a certain sort of telepathic engagement as another avenue of
acquiring knowledge.

Born in Los Angeles, I spent the first ten years of my life
happily in California where I skateboarded or biked my way to
school. On the way home I honed my life-long fascination for
flowers, picking just the tops off to give to my mom, who always
asked what happened to the stems.

Joined by my adoring Greek-American family we walked

through the orange groves behind our house outside Santa Barbara and I raced my dad down sidewalks lined with cherry trees in bloom. My father is an inventor and painter. My grandparents, also immigrants from Greece, liked to pick olives and brine them in the garage. My dad drove them out of town to collect walnuts and the herbs my grandmother knew how to identify. Meanwhile I explored every reach of the divine Santa Barbara county landscape.

Brigitte, my mother's best friend, was a member of our close extended friendship family. We went on many camping trips with her and her family. She taught me how to swim and through her I learned about the arcane subject of death. When I was five I found a wounded butterfly and took it inside, built a box for it to recover in and brought it grass clippings. Innocence was lost three days later as I asked Brigitte why it didn't live. The beautiful, peaceful world I thought I lived in was turned on its head. I remember thinking it's just unfair.

Even at the tender age of seven I remember learning about Vietnam. The violence of it shocked me. I could not believe that something so heinous and cowardly had actually taken place in the world. For me it spelled the descent of a civilization. It seemed out of place in the natural order and when I thought of it I felt a red and black whirlpool reverberating in the air around me. Death and destruction. Chaos. I was a child and I was coming to grips with a world that doesn't always make sense.

I was so grateful to believe I would live in a generation that would not have to experience the kind of evil, unjustified brutality that kills young hearts. I remember hoping that my lifetime would be an era of peace, because that meant the world to me—to be safe and to live in a just world.

I exhibited an uncanny ability to hone in on lost objects. An unidentifiable source seemed to put a key in the lock, opening my brain to vital information—directing me, almost magnetically—to it.

I was oddly knowledgeable of measurements of all sorts, particularly spatially and rarely arithmetically—when sometimes large sums of numbers popped into my head sparing me the arduous pain of a homework math problem.

I was a wonder with repairing electronic appliances, often knowing exactly which part of the equipment needed adjusting. Sometimes it just took a touch of my hands to restore it. Even from an early age I needed to put this ability to use. I wanted to rectify what was wrong in an environment. These may have been early splashes of intuition at work. As things would turn out, my mind had a mind of its own. *I* was just along for the ride.

I recognized even at a young age that this was beyond what was conventionally possible, but in each development, those who noticed were too pre-occupied to see it as a separate trait— just a fluke.

Once I moved to the Midwest with my mother, there weren't any out-and-out paranormal happenings. I didn't see dead people. Except perhaps once. I was thirteen at the time. I was sitting on the edge of my bed when a vision appeared to me. The apparition had long, wavy sandy-blond hair, deep soulful loving bluish eyes and a tunic-type dress. He was surrounded by some kind of atmospheric bubble I had no words to explain. I have only recently learned that this is called a *nimbus*.

The image hovered in my room for several seconds: *He was seeing me.* There was an energy conveying the sense that this was someone who knew me and who was shepherding me into something. He smiled.

In that one and only waking vision, I knew I was headed for something—what, I had no idea. I just knew I was different some-how and my life would not be the same as others. I was separate with my senses and vision. With myriad supernatural occurrences like this, my youth shaped into an apocalyptic adolescence.

In my mid-teens I had run-of-the-mill psychic dreams, including dreams of forewarnings, but I didn't realize my psychic senses were beyond average until my uncanny pre-cognitive dreams set in with regularity. I often dreamt these in *real time* as if catapulted on scene. Let me take you into one of my dreams…

In a ferocious fight between earth and sky, a tornado pummels through a city, its location clearly marked by a green highway sign.

When I jolted awake the word "*Tuscaloosa*" was repeatedly skittering across my tongue. It was important I remember it. I knew this dream was telling me something.

Within an hour of awaking, I watched a tornado blast through Tuscaloosa, Alabama in real life on the morning news. Holy moly! I was having dreams that were foretelling the future of the world—about places I'd never even known to exist. These pre-cognitive dreams were *uniquely real* to me; they took on an entire dimension of their own. (This was a tornado that occurred during my teens, not the one that happened recently in the same area. Looking back, there tends to be a "double-whammy" effect regarding locations.)

> *I first read the draft of Rebecca's book in late 2010, in which she recounted the dream she had of a tornado touching down in Tuscaloosa, months before the deadly tornado in April of 2011.*
>
> —Michele Pollock

Throughout my high school years I became confident that I had abilities, but faced a dilemma because I understood that they were often not appreciated or easily understood. Nonetheless, I started to make amazing predictions regarding peoples' lives. I was not asked to—it was more like I was told.

I received the first message of impending warning when I

was around 17. Sitting alone on the edge of my bed, I was made aware—like a telepathic nudge—that a man the family knew was going to be involved in an automobile wreck *the following day*.

I "heard" it all subliminally, in a single moment, as if remembering something somebody had told me. I was amazed at how completely natural, yet somber it felt. It was an experience so real that it was unmistakable as anything other.

Concerned, I rushed to inform the man's father. It was the first time, but not the last, that I was greeted by blasé disbelief. He barely looked up from the television screen while I sternly recited my warning. But I *had* to.

Like clockwork, the next day, the man wrecked his truck. *I knew when I knew.* The emotion involved was powerful, compelling me to use my voice. As it turned out, the driver walked away skidding off the state highway to avoid hitting a deer, totaling his truck.

His father plainly sighed—perhaps dumfounded, "You'll never live that one down." Well, I'm all grown up now, and in hindsight, that's easier said than done. But I had been ignored beforehand. This could have been life-saving information!

I am glad I spoke up about it, without fear of being labeled or doubting the message given me. Was I being tested? Loved ones from beyond are looking out for us and do want us to stay safe. But first, they have to get their messages across.

In another remarkable dream, I experienced what felt like a *visitation* from a couple from our family's past, unusual in appearance and dressed in a particular way that was unfamiliar to me until verified later through photographs. They had passed away; yet, as if we needed to introduce ourselves to each other, we met by some inexplicable means at the same place where time is stationary. This is thought to be a psychic-mediumistic experience, which many people have experienced. This dream helped expand my reality, showing me that, in our dreams, connections over great distances are not impossible, and that some part of our consciousness or soul survives death.

On a smaller scale I began earning my "psi-legs" by paying attention to little signs that might be messages placed in a synchronistic fashion. I was engaging and learning psychically from my environment, much as an infant learns to speak. Instead of cutting it off, I was paying attention to its workings.

While riding in the car with my friend David, I bashfully confided, "I'm psychic...your car's name is 'Janet'!" I was scared to tell him, as if it were the most taboo pronouncement, but I had to let it out.

Instead of derisive laughter he replied, "That was amazing." He had never even shared that he indeed had a name for his car—Janet. The rest of that car ride, David and I considered all the intriguing aspects of the powers of the mind. We discussed that eerie feeling you get when you have your back turned, and yet can feel someone is looking at you and your senses become alerted, switching on a reflex to turn around. Unless we have eyes in the back of our heads, this feeling is a result of a different sense, and it *must be innate* if we can feel it without even trying.

Not all manifestations of my prickly senses were pleasant. I was unwilling to wear a piece of clothing after I had worn it in stress-filled public environments, like high school classrooms, until it was washed. At the end of the day, when I touched it I was repelled by feelings of emotional stress that had become absorbed into the fabric, clinging to the material like a layer of psychic cooties. I didn't know what this all-absorption process was defined as until ten years later when I ran across the word "psychometry."

Returning home one afternoon, I noticed our pet collie sitting on the front steps of our house. A cloud of emotion cut so deep into my own senses that without even thinking I could feel what the dog was feeling. I asked my mother point blank: "Did the cat die?" Tiger Lilly, a Manx cat, was older, but had not previously shown signs of any acute illness.

"Yes," my mother replied, but I already knew for myself that it was true. Though I didn't realize it at the time, this was an inkling of my ability to discern the inner feelings of animals.

One afternoon sitting in a classroom, I experienced a jolt—someone was going through my room at home! I left class, shaken and outraged, and called home. Before anyone answered, I hung up. What was I going to say? When I got home, I found that someone had rummaged through my room and taken something vital to me—a space heater. Someone had invaded my space and I could remotely feel it. A warning was going off inside me—my developing senses were working to protect me.

I could not have foreseen how this particular event was just the start.

> *My testimonial is about Rebecca giving a reading to me, and my dog coming up as one of the first things. She was so dead-on with my pet. She knew details and specifics about my dog that only my family would know because we live with her. She knew that she was allergic to specific items and that her right paw had problems. She also knew that she has a yeast problem in her left ear. It was so interesting.*
>
> —Shannon

More jarring manifestations of my ESP were to follow. On December 7, 1988, before the news officially broke to me, I announced to a classmate: "*There was an earthquake in the Ukraine.*" I felt like a human seismograph. Next I sensed that there would be about 40,000 people killed. I had to say something to *someone*! (This would become the biggest problem for me on down the road. Who would be the person to share these predictions with?)

Later that day I heard NBC news anchorman Dan Rather report:

> *These are the ruins of Leninakan, in the central square of the town shows the exact time the earthquake struck. The second largest city in Armenia is in ruins. We saw houses turned into heaps of metal and concrete. Schools and kindergartens turned into heaps of rubble. We saw people—their faces full of grief and anguish and tragedy you cannot express in words. According to preliminary estimates the earthquake of unprecedented strength destroyed two thirds of the city of Leninakan. The city of Spitak, 70 km away, a population of more than 20,000 has been practically wiped from the face of the earth. Overall in the disaster-stricken area hundreds of thousands have been made homeless and tens of thousands lost their lives.*

(Although I had felt the word "Ukraine" and the earthquake happened in Armenia, these two countries are in the same geographic area and were both part of the same Soviet bloc.)

Since then I've been bombarded with details from the ether about virtually anyone or anything, anytime. These days I can usually pick up when someone is thinking of me. I can often perceive who and I can feel the emotions behind the line of thought. This is not surprising, considering that modern science indicates that thoughts are forms of energy. It also illustrates that one's thoughts or whereabouts, given a quality psychic's abilities of receiving, are never completely secret or private.

I found it particularly frustrating that when reading newspaper articles, I could sense when facts were misconstrued and when liars had infiltrated the political system. I found myself filling in the blanks between lines of reported newsprint, providing information missing in unsolved cases. I found, if used properly, my intuitions could be life-saving.

This placed me in a profound conundrum. For years I battled an urgency to speak with those in authority—someone who might be able to use my abilities to stop suffering. But who? What if I poured out my heart to them and they didn't believe in psychics?

Throughout the ensuing years, I have pushed myself, seeking out many responsible authority figures, fervently giving demonstrations and explaining my pre-cognitive dreams. I found an associate pastor who believed in my abilities and suggested I help the police. So I spoke with a chief of detectives regarding a missing person's case. I recounted for him a dream that would come true a few years later. At the time I didn't know what I was up against—green to the outside world at broaching this subject and the implications of it. I had to fight to get people to keep both ears open to listen. I knew I must use my abilities to serve.

Once, I even risked safe harbor of being an anonymous citizen and dared to speak with the F.B.I. I described, again and again, to all the people I could think of, one specific, fateful dream—a dream so significant, in fact, that when it came true it directly affected people around the world.

Just when I was on the precipice of dreaming this fateful dream, it is noteworthy that I was planning to get married. The last name of my fiancé? The very name I intuited over a decade earlier. We lived at 911 N. Madison, a "shotgun" style house purchased for him by his father, a former Air Force drill sergeant. (I would come to recognize that this number would later manifest itself everywhere around me.)

In my experience psychic dreams and insights can prove to be a form of patriotism. They can bridge an important gap in the structure of securing our nation; they can help our citizenry.

❀ 2 Awakening

*Homer's <u>Odyssey</u> is like the ashes of a great
fire—so much has been lost in translation.*
—Professor Germanakos

I was unready for college and my mother learned of a very special
program: Ithaca Mentor Semester in Greece. My mother was in
President Kennedy's first group of Peace Corps volunteers and
believed in understanding other cultures. I wanted to attend
mainly to learn Greek language and history, but I never imagined
what this five-month journey would accomplish. A fellow student
referred to it as an intellectual boot camp. All ten students hailed
from the best private schools on the east coast and were preparing
for Ivy League educations. A few couldn't take it and left, one
being retrieved on location courtesy of his dad's helicopter escort.

We lived in a home with our mentors on the island of Evvia,
a cold, windy little peninsula where only the hardiest tourists
venture. I studied harder than I ever have, before or since. Our
time was precious there. To ensure we didn't waste any time, we
were allowed to shower for five minutes once a week only. We
scrubbed our clothes by hand in the back yard with cold water.
We rotated helping with the cooking. And love was created by
such an immersion into something distinctly different from all
the distractions of our previous lax culture.

We worked from dawn 'till dusk in the classroom and all week for families in the community. It was a communal experience; we learned the custom dances and performed at night accompanied by local musicians. If you could only hear this music in person in some far away hilly "taverna" on a Greek island you would be made anew. I promise. On Saturdays we would go on marathon hikes over mountains—literally eight hours at a stretch—all over Greece, exploring and learning from the changing environment. We traveled to incorporate what we were learning in the classroom.

Our tutelage came from the best of minds—visiting professors from around the world, including two highly regarded archaeologists—those who are called in when, in places that are under construction in Egypt, mummies are uncovered. We studied language, art, history, poetry, and music, all connected with first-hand accounts. Given different exercises, we were to try harder than ever to grow independently, to develop the might of our minds.

Bathed in this massive light of knowledge, I came into my own.

On one island we scaled a monument of a thousand steps. We explored the city of Tinos, where miracles are said to occur. I ran on the track where the first Olympics were held. The food alone was enough to change anyone's sense of life. Rich, aromatic, lemony salads and heavenly desserts were customary everywhere we went. It took years to wean myself from the unique tangy decadence of the hand-crafted coffee.

If you are ever seeking a spiritual conversion or experience come to a town such as this—steeped in tradition, observe their Easter celebration as everybody gathers as one to hike the island over, a few bearing the cross as they go. I can't imagine a more hospitable region of the world. When I traveled around Greece, experiencing the museums and ruins something awakened in me: The ruins around the Acropolis, the timeless mystique of marble-strewn beaches, art and classic history that feeds the origins of our own democracy were all literally at my fingertips. Everything came together at once. Life is intricate. It can have incomprehensible beauty and poetry. All of this changed my way of thinking; you might say it changed my mortal soul. I saw what I needed to see for the first time.

This was my coming-of-age, my rite of passage. Like the Parthenon herself, I reached new heights, becoming "enlightened." I think that this journey made my body, mind and soul come together as never before. It triggered in me independent thinking and broader analysis and fostered perception. The gift was not the program; the gift was that the program resurrected my mind.

Even though I knew I had unexplained psychic experiences, it was never mystifying to me—just part of my normal, natural existence. Things were only getting started.

One day back at home, out of nowhere, I felt I was traveling through a tunnel. In essence it was like being re-born. Next thing I knew, I felt healed and one hundred percent transformed as a person. A joy resonated through my heart like never before.

From then on, I began to experience the world and the way living things resonated with me on a heightened level. I remember being near a field and sensing each blade of grass as though it were singing. Nature became a powerful, sentient, emotive, living landscape, not just passing scenery. I sensed its intrinsic compassion towards us as a healing resource in our lives.

There *is* more. It might be out of grasp of our central eyes, but never out of touch to our hearts. I would *never* have believed this could happen to anyone until it happened to me. I was new. My senses had awakened as if they had been in a deep sleep!

Though raised in a non-religious household, something

fresh—divine—was beginning to percolate in and lift up my soul as well. I had no reliable basis to believe in God. Until right then I did not believe in the soul. I thought that was all akin to folklore. I only saw people who abused that tradition or who spent all their energy in cruel ways to castigate people who don't fit in.

After a few more personal, revelatory experiences stirred me to realize that this is really not a soulless, spiritually-devoid plane of existence, I had a great desire to heal people. The catch was I had no idea how I would do that.

My inner faith was to be pure, private, and not tainted by the societal ignorance of prejudice. Something *had* touched my soul and I wouldn't lose sight of that, though it became more easily said than done when churning about in the misery of the "real" world.

I could not be segregated from society like a monk. Though I had changed, the rest of the world was still the same. It was nearly impossible to keep up the "good vibrations" day-in-day-out with no one with whom I could share these developing, profound experiences. And no matter what I was doing I continued to have a steady stream of predictive dreams. I didn't grow out of it; I grew into it.

❧ 3 A Fateful Dream

A dream un-interpreted is like a letter left unopened.

—Talmud

To receive psychic insight while awake, I usually have to make a concentrated effort. Not so for dreams. As the mind is in this neutral gear, dreams are very fertile ground for psychic proceedings. The brain—on psychic-autopilot—does the work for you.

Sometime in the fall of 1992, I had a fateful dream:

In the blue sky, three small military fighter jets are being flown individually by Middle Eastern looking men who speak in French or with distinctly French accents. In a concerted effort, each of these planes is flown into the bottom section of two adjacent skyscrapers.

These are sister skyscrapers. One tower has a huge thin point sticking out on top. They are located along a big-city street in a metropolitan area full of other tall buildings. Jagged spikes of steel stand out from a mushrooming cloud of black dust.

When I awoke, I knew for certain that what I had seen in this dream was going to happen in the future. I was *totally* sure. This was a warning dream. The essence of the dream was one I had become accustomed to, with a very real feeling of impending urgency. I was convinced it would come to pass.

At this time in my life nothing else mattered as much as

my predictions. My life was on stand-by for these dreams. I was simply some kind of bridge. I was desperate to find some way to record my predictions and to pass this warning along to the authorities, but I was afraid they would consider me a real kook. I wrote down the dream in preparation of handing it over. I knew someone needed to know. I had to tell people what I saw so it might be prevented. What would they do with it? How could I just burst into a police station with this kind of prediction?

I sat, antsy and uncomfortable, in my parked car, deliberating a long time about what measures to take, whether or not to turn in my hand-scrawled prediction. Finally, I crumpled the paper into a ball, started my car and just let it all go. Some weeks passed.

At that time I had no knowledge of what these buildings in my dream were, or in what city they were even located. The only New York City landmark I could readily recognize was the Statue of Liberty. All that I remember learning about the financial district in school was that my birthday, October 29th, demarcates the first crash of the New York Stock Exchange (causing the great depression).

Then, in February 1993, the basement of the World Trade Center was bombed. I had confirmation that my dream had serious psychic significance to our nation, and I learned precisely the name and location of the tall twin towers in my dream.

Given the type of attack and its location, I postulated that what had just happened was the end of the story. I felt that my pre-cognitive dream had come to pass with eerie similarity, though not 100 percent accuracy as to the method of strike. It would be another eight and a half years before the rest of my prophetic dream played itself out.

❀ 4 Princess and the Pea

Conversion for me was not a Damascus Road experience. I slowly moved into an intellectual acceptance of what my intuition had always known.

—Madeleine L'Engle

Wherever I go, my psychic ability follows. In 1998 I went to work for a law firm as a title searcher, applying for the job solely because I liked to find things. I couldn't have anticipated it would be working at the courthouse where I would find my long-awaited test subjects. Working here—in this case—was "meant to be."

One day I hesitantly revealed I was "psychic." My co-workers wanted demonstrations! They had to know more, to see it for themselves. Phillip, a former stylist, was my first test subject. I don't know where this came from—I had never heard of the sense of psychic touch before—but I felt the urge to touch his boot.

When I did, I began reciting the most unusual details about the people in his life and very specific situations he was encountering. Whoa!! He turned pale in astonishment and his well-coifed hair seemed to stand on end. This special kind of intuitive sense just took off for me like wildfire—a latent discovery.

That day, I told people the most amazing things going on in their lives and the lives of those they knew, just from holding onto various objects they presented to me. Holding onto a ring of one of my older co-workers, Christie, I told her the exact name of the decades-old song she had been singing the night before and described the objects she had been selecting for Christmas presents by *brand name*. And this was practice!

I also noticed I was able to pick up on particular medical problems just by speaking to someone. This was incredible beginner's luck, as they say, because no one had shown me how any of this works. It was truly mind-blowing and very magical. After the impromptu demos, people were stunned by what they had just experienced. They didn't need to understand it; they knew it was special. And it was so natural to me that I didn't stop to analyze everything going on. I just kept doing what I do.

Here's an account of one of those psychometry readings. Lenora was a petite blond college student at the time, studying geology. She was interested and excited about her object reading. We walked into a private alcove, surrounded by the architectural grandeur of the courthouse foyer's marble columns. I loved spending my days there in that atmosphere. She smiled in anticipation as I held onto one of her rings. I explained she'd had an argument and gave the word "Colgate." Her blue eyes widened as she confirmed she and her roommate had just had a quarrel that morning over the Colgate toothpaste.

Next, I said that her boyfriend's brother had just been released from jail after a three-day incarceration. Right. Then I described the unusual mode of transportation to his destination—by train. I knew nothing about her innermost private life, or if her boyfriend even had a brother. But to backtrack his footsteps to the day? She was reeling from my command performance.

In the midst of this, I discovered I had true psychic mediumship abilities. I was sitting next to Christie one day when there was a knock at the door of my mind. "Who's there?" I gasped silently.

Christie's husband was trying to communicate with her through me. I took a leap of faith and asked Christie if her husband was deceased, then continued with my nudged inspiration.

The first time you realize that you are communicating with the dead, it actually feels enlivening. It was spiritual and it came forth in a healing, helpful context. But, after this exchange he wouldn't let me be. It felt like a big responsibility to help heal his pain by communicating with his loved ones—he had a huge Irish family. He seemed to be stuck with unresolved issues and it was wearing on me emotionally. I had my own life and needed to protect my own emotional space. When I shared this with Christie, she smiled, satisfied, and acknowledged that it was just like him not to leave people alone.

As soon as I requested that he "knock it off," he simply went away for good.

This proved to me that I could have one-on-one communication with someone from beyond without sight or physical presence. The experience was much more significant to me than just holding onto objects to feel things about a person. It was a tremendous outlet for guiding and healing people.

The more I tried to process the meanings of this manner of communication—both delicate and demanding—I knew my life had changed. Again. Of my abilities, this was the most vexing for me to simply accept. Seemingly without my trying I had just been "enrolled" in a new category of sense that seemed to transcend them all. It was useful, but did I really want this?

Right around this time, I awoke from a peaceful slumber to a telepathic awareness:

You are a messenger. You are here to re-unite the lost with the living.

Though silent, the message was intense enough to rouse me from bed. Mesmerized, I could feel the truth of it, as though it originated from a pure source. Things were all starting to make sense. There was a gentle but just power that does not come from me but gets translated through my senses.

I was so relieved! There was undoubtedly a higher calling behind what I've been given. It's not just a party diversion. It's as real as real can get.

That was the first and last time I received a directive. The rest is history.

There are times when I am alone that important and deeply desperate people come through to me and relate various things. They can source me, as if I have some type of invisible beacon. I can't help it. I am a medium, and the deceased know. They know how to find me, as if they have a directory. This actually causes me some pain. My senses can never be shut down, so I can always read. When I'm there, they're there. This forces me into a position of duty, not leisure.

> *My favorite visit to Rebecca would have to be after my brother passed. Rebecca was able to connect with him. She gave me details of the night he passed, including who was in the room. It was a huge comfort to me to be able to communicate with him...Every time I go to see Rebecca he comes through. I feel very blessed to have this connection.*
>
> *— S. Adams*

When I am out and about the deceased often manage to get through to me in hopes I will connect them to their living family members in the vicinity. To me, this proves they are not in some static place known as "Heaven" all day long, looking down on us via some type of celestial satellite network. They, or some part of their souls' makeup, are out and about with us too. And they have a crushing need to pass on urgent messages about upcoming big life changes or health issues, or to simply say they miss someone.

A lot. In other words, they are still very much alive, only in a different way.

One day Christie's older sister showed up at work because she was consumed with anxiety over her upcoming bladder surgery. She was afraid she would die during the operation. I knew she was looking for information from me, the newly-discovered seer.

I was overwhelmed by her pain. I felt physically sick and had to quickly leave. I couldn't handle it. I didn't want to feel the energy of her problems. When I read for people I absorb all their emotions and suffering. For me, a reading can go on a long time after the client is gone. The feelings get under my skin and I continue to receive impressions about their problems. It can become a little too intimate.

Later, after I'd had some breathing room, I shared with Christie that her sister's surgery would go very well. "She is quite fortunate to have the best surgeon for her case. In two weeks, however, the stitches are going to come loose and she will need to return to the doctor."

That is exactly what happened—to the day. It was good information and I believed I helped her. The weird thing about it? I didn't really even *try*. It just passed from my lips without conscious thought. What I also learned that day was that her sister did not need to be present for me to receive information about her. Without meditation or having an object of hers to hold, I was able to foretell an event in the woman's future.

I have a knack for ticking off future events. This has been a mainstay of my life. Sometimes the mood just hits me. I don't know how, since these "super" abilities don't come embedded with a handy instruction manual. Instead, they surface like any other natural instinct.

Too many of these kinds of events—more than I can detail—

have happened for them to be mere coincidences. And now I don't believe there is a *maximum capacity* for all things psychic.

This 'touchiness' I have—the *inability* to close myself off from receiving messages and impressions, is a double-edged sword for me. In my past I had to sell or give away items in my home that absorbed negative energy. If it bothers me, I can't simply ignore it; I am psychically impressionable to objects and the energy of my environment.

While I was getting used to these impressions and feelings and starting to recognize them as normal for me in my mid-twenties, some experiences managed to catch me off-guard.

Being a psychic is sometimes like leaving one world and entering another. I was at Waikiki Beach. As I entered the ocean surf I felt and sensed a feeling of desperation, chaos and grief encircling me from the sailors who had perished not too far away in Pearl Harbor. It was like I was in a minefield of souls. I have since learned that energy seeks to heal itself. Peril that strong has not washed away with time. I don't mean to say that their souls were trapped there, but snippets of the energy of the event still lingered, exposed. All I could do to find out more, to understand what was happening, was to reach out to it. But I was still not "activated" as a psychic, so I had no frame of reference in which to place this holographic-like scene that I had breached. I was not ready for this.

When I was a teenager, I chatted with my friends about the "miracle sense" of clairvoyance. I remember thinking to myself, *Wow! The ability to see things at a distance, how incredible!* I wanted to do it myself, but assumed that because I hadn't, I couldn't. I believed, even then, it was a rare and precious skill. *Clairvoyants could do anything,* I thought—like solve crimes.

I was getting bits and pieces of data psychically, but it was out of my voluntary control. ESP would come on erratically to warn me or to guide me, sometimes during my sleep. Most of these were passive, unveiling experiences to me. I was unseasoned in manipulating it to work more powerfully for me.

One of my earlier clairvoyant experiences happened one day before work. A video-like montage—dark and stormy at the center and surrounded by a cloudy border—struck me hard emotionally. This was a new "set of specs" for me to experience being awake. I envisioned that a young man would be hired at our law firm and it would be the wrong choice. My job was my world and I had a respectful working relationship with these good attorneys.

I urgently wanted to call our main attorney and warn him: *you are about to hire a young man. Don't.* But then I would have to explain myself and my premonition—that I was a psychic. I wasn't prepared for that. I was not especially eager to be separated out from the crowd of "regular" employees. Until then, I played it safe by explaining any heightened-type perceptions as women's intuition. That's an easy cover.

Low-and-behold, later that very day, I was informed a 24-year-old male paralegal from the East Coast was to be our firm's newest hire. His employment would turn out to be semi-disastrous. He made my life miserable with his bombasts, cussing, and the legal snafus he caused.

After this episode, clairvoyance—that very mystical sense— seemed a possibility for me. Some might say, when you least expect it, expect it. In this particular case, when I needed to be forewarned a vision came unexpectedly.

I never considered myself a "misfit" socially. But I am a fairly quiet person. I have always been grateful that I was spared from literally hearing voices or seeing spirits floating around. But that doesn't mean I am understood. The man with whom I was involved most of my life never understood nor believed in psychics. Believe me, I tried. I knew I had to meet him on his level, to introduce my abilities to him in a context he could understand.

We were by ourselves watching a Hoosier basketball game. As so it happens I was having a surge that day in my precognitive command. I started telling him exactly what was going to happen next in the game: sudden changes, who would score, when and how it would end.

He grew excited about this sports-related

> *Over the years I have found my readings with Rebecca incredible; each spot on with whatever happens to be going on in my life at the moment. A few months ago Rebecca told me that I would have to change jobs at work and that this had to do with a man at work, but that it would only be temporary and would actually feel somewhat like a break to me. I told her during my reading that that was unlikely as I'm the person in charge during my shift and because of my home life I would not be able to change shifts. Also, my field is female dominated so in the moment my job having something to do with a man did not make much sense to me. Rebecca simply reiterated that this is what she saw. However, soon after this reading the man in charge of a different unit but still in our dept. and on my same shift had to have surgery and I was the person qualified to work his unit which I ended up doing for about a month. And the change did feel like a break to me. I laughed when this situation unfolded because I honestly did not see how what Rebecca predicted could possibly happen but it did.*
>
> —Dawn

feat. He could hardly believe what he was hearing and seeing and I made him a convert. But he was born in the tiny town of Worthington, Indiana and before me had never tried anything remotely foreign to him, including eating an avocado, and the psychic arena was highly unfamiliar territory for him. He was even afraid of wearing men's sandals and going sock-less. Despite what I had demonstrated during the basketball game, it was easier for him to revert to his natural skeptical state. But, every now and then he would bring it up out of the blue, vociferously reliving each and every "predictive score" I had made. But for him it was one of those things he didn't care to understand so he buried it away.

Frustrated that my earth-shattering insights were always ignored, the breaking point finally came. Sometimes when I get "charged up," it's like I put the pedal-to-the metal with my abilities. (I'll show you...!) I tossed out a doozy of a forecast for him: *"Tomorrow you are going to find gold and trip and hurt your ankle."* The next day, while walking his dog, he dropped his car keys. When he bent to retrieve them, he found a gold-colored bottle cap that spelled "gold" on top. He picked it up. On the way back to his car, he tripped and hurt his ankle. Though he admitted several days later what had happened, the whole nature of it was unsettling to him. But even if he were convinced, he never would have really "listened." And he could never comprehend the value my abilities have for society, which was something of the gravest importance to me in my life.

Even my closest family members were tough to convince.

My grandmother ordered a couch and I was with her when she called to find out the delivery status. They told her it was not scheduled to arrive for four more weeks. I chimed in: "It will be here on Thursday." Turns out I was right; it was delivered that very Thursday! She remembered my prediction later in wonderment, yet, even so, she didn't want to believe there was anything extraordinary to it. It just didn't "fit" with what she had been taught in her lifetime. No one can tell the future, right? Well, I can. It's a gift. It's a trait. But I was on my own.

Though ESP is both innate and commonly experienced, the mind and its connection to our bodies and our souls is a very complicated thing to express. I could see and feel things totally inconceivable to anyone else, including my family. Even if I tried to show them—tried to help them understand where I was coming from—they could not appreciate it by means of their regular senses. You can't get away from the evidence of my, and others' supplementary senses, but you can deny them. When I ignore my intuition, I pay for it. When others ignore my intuition they pay for it, too. The sixth sense can be lifesaving and it should not be stigmatized.

I knew my gift could serve altruistic purposes and I remained undeterred. In my heart of hearts, I wanted to use my abilities to help people. I decided to take the lead by contacting the authorities and offering my services. It was no easy task.

I called the local F.B.I. agency where I lived. When I asked the woman who answered the phone if they ever worked with psychics, she laughed like a hyena. I was astounded by the unprofessional response from what I considered to be a professional federal agency. If these were the authorities I needed to work with, it was going to be a long road to find a way to put my abilities to real use for society. Though that slowed me down, it did not stop me.

❧ 5 Predictions Process

It lies with our Lord to make revelations to
whom He pleases.

        —Joan of Arc: In Her Own Words

For a long time I searched for someone to whom I could explain my predictive phenomena, someone who would take me seriously and not brush me off. I needed someone with that faultless, appreciative sense of love in his or her heart and who was willing to listen. At least I would then have *someone* with whom I could share my predictions, especially things on the horizon to which we were all vulnerable.

I thought I had finally found this person, a casual friend for whom I had informally read in the past. I told her how I can feel events before they happen—that something beyond my awareness simply begins feeding information to me, without my trying. As I was explaining the process to her, right there in her presence, a new prediction was born within me. My voice quavered and my stomach quivered as I told her, "I am certain that terrorists are going to attack our schools—in October." When you're like me you need to get your message out, sometimes to just about anyone who can take the burden off your shoulders.

When I feel the onset of a tragic event, or violence somewhere in the world I get a sickening feeling. I don't know how these feelings are communicated to me. I don't understand the biological process, but it is enough to cause a pronounced, real physiological effect.

The intuition was strong, moving me nearly to the point of tears. Previously in America there had been a few dispersed attacks, such as Columbine, but nothing in a long time. My friend couldn't help me, but at least she listened.

A week or two later, beginning in October, just as I had said, a string of five school shootings happened, practically back-to-back. It was unprecedented the way they occurred one after another. My prediction came true. My awareness interprets the word attacker and terrorist as one and the same. It's notable that I don't have a history of calling people about things that never end up happening. If I have a premonition strong enough to prompt me to call family or friends to talk about it, two or three days later the event happens. Now when I have a dream about a plane crash, I know it's significant and likely to happen somewhere. For example, in 2004 I woke up from a dream where I saw a jetliner making a crash descent. Three letters were emblazoned on its side. I was certain it was going to happen. I was very nervous about it. I called my best friend and my mom to tell them. Three days later a plane crashed that went by an acronym with only one letter difference.

Sometimes my intuitions come when I am alone, giving me information that opposes current news or pollsters. Sometimes it is influenced by whom I am with. I'm not totally perfect, nor do I strive for perfection. This is a natural, as opposed to contrived occurrence. I am living my life when inspirations zap into my brain unannounced. These intercepts are often in the right ballpark, but that doesn't always guarantee I completely perceive the signal.

For example, after the initial attacks in London on 7/7/2005, I tuned up my ESP radar, so to speak, and instantly knew that *another attack would occur in two weeks*. I emailed this to my mom. Again, I had to send it out there to someone—anyone. I sensed it would be in Rome this time. The attack did come, exactly when I predicted, but it occurred in London once again.

In August, 2001, when Iraq was not yet publicly on anyone's radar screen and no one was talking about Saddam Hussein, I wrote down that he would somehow "cause" a decomposition of most of the Middle East. I wrote that it would happen halfway through 2003. It happened earlier than that, but it *did* happen. The time frame, however, that I predicted was when Saddam Hussein was captured. Certain messages come through in a sketchy way.

For a psychic, a picture really *is* worth a thousand words. Days before the 2004 election, when I saw George W. Bush on television with his wife following a few paces behind him, I picked up an exact insight that told me everything I needed to know about the election. I knew the *exact margin* by which he would win the election. The exit poll predictions, which actually forecasted the reverse, had nothing on me.

I do *not* read articles, study events or anything else to "get" a psychic revelation. I just pick up the vibes in a matter of a moment. It's like I taste it on the tip of my tongue. And all at once I want to tell the world. My mother did not believe me for a second when I foretold this truth—it was truly inconceivable given the current pulse of the nation beating so strongly for his opponent. Therefore, when it actually happened it wasn't relevant enough for her to remember. She had discounted it. However, one of her guests at a party remembered precisely what I uttered, and has talked about it since. She later became a client.

> *Update: I had my most recent reading January 2012. I wanted information regarding my grandson's upcoming visit to Mexico City as an exchange student [for three weeks]. Rebecca stated that there would be an earthquake while he was there and that communications would be out of service for a while. Just found out that there was a 7.6 magnitude earthquake in Mexico that was felt in Mexico City. Communications are indeed down as we have been trying to call for the past hour. Hard to imagine a more accurate prediction.*
>
> —Dianne Saffron

Again, I don't ever try to "think it out" beforehand. The information simply comes to me like a telegraph from an unknown station.

Like this: In 2006 while on the phone with my father I felt a message of caution come up from nowhere, which I passed along to my dad. Things coming to us from China would soon start making us sick. A handful of months later a slew of Chinese imports were being recalled: Aqua Dots, toys with lead paint, poisonous carp, and eventually melamine-laced pet food and baby formula. My predictions are usually timely and safety-related, otherwise there would be no reason to pick up on them. If anyone was really interested and willing to listen I was able to forecast events in the future.

But those who didn't or couldn't take it seriously would make my efforts seem like throwing water on fire. Some element like oxygen would be missing, as if another's acceptance or tolerance can cause a reaction—or deactivation of my senses. There has to be some forthright, earnest commitment from my participant witness.

In order to be taken seriously in the future, I needed a way to prove my predictions. The problem was that as time passes, peoples' memories get hazy about what predictions you shared with them, they feigned listening to begin with, or they are hesitant to vouch for me because they feel embarrassed. In the end, the responsibility of backing up my predictions lies in my hands alone. And by this time in my life, this special sight had recognizably serious implications.

I needed to create my own place in a world that officially has no place for me to belong.

In 2007, I came across a website, www.Prophecies.us, where one is able to officially record predictions. If only I had found this way back when! The site seemed to be full of people who were making "outlandish" predictions about alien destruction, but I ignored all the end-of-our-days scenarios and plucked away at the keyboard. For a moment I finally found a place where my voice registered in the world, even if it was only a URL. But it wasn't all joy. Submitting my predictions to a computer took away part of the human touch. It felt artificial and it gutted the spontaneity of prediction. I was poor so I didn't own a home computer or have a smart phone. It wasn't the ultimate solution to proving my predictions, but it was totally free and open when and if I wanted to put up with the rigmarole of sitting in a cordoned-off library room with grimy keyboards, which wasn't often.

In early 2007 I went ahead and transferred several of my predictions for U.S. politics in the upcoming 2008 elections onto the website from the piece of torn-up envelope on which I had hastily scrawled them. The following is how it went.

At the time Rudy Giuliani was the clear front-runner for the Republican presidential nomination, and was leading in the polls, but I predicted instead that he would withdraw—amid scandal.

John McCain seemed to be at the end of his rope, out of campaign money and laying off staff, but again, right at that time I predicted he would win the Republican presidential nomination.

Everyone was saying America was not ready for an African-American president. But when I asked myself, *who will the next president be,* I intuited "blackmail—or was it "black male?" Telepathically, it is impossible to distinguish between such homonyms, and in the world of politics, it could literally be either word. Though I did not get the name "Obama," which would have helped me out, for a long time I was still sure Obama would prevail.

One day after, I happened to be watching a short-lived talk show hosted by a bald psychiatrist, featuring a pair of psychic sisters who relayed about the upcoming election: "We don't think America is ready for a black president." I actually yelled in defiance, knowing they were wrong about their prediction. I even told a trusted friend I knew Obama would win, but as a Clinton supporter, she couldn't accept that. So, what if I was reading it wrong?

So I changed my mind—swayed by opinion, abridging my perception that the word must actually be "blackmail." I had grown cynical enough, since our political process was dragged through so much mud lately, to believe the message I was getting foretold scandal.

Here's something I've learned: now when I make predictions, I don't think and I don't second-guess myself. It destroys the process. I missed the mark when I ignored my true, first impression and tried to "handle" it. It's only necessary to receive the impressions, not color them by prevailing attitudes.

Still, I made some uncanny, intriguing prognostications about the presidential race. Hillary Clinton was way ahead of Barack Obama at the time. Clinton was universally expected to tie things up early in the spring, since the race wasn't even close. But I predicted that Obama and Clinton would be "*neck and neck— almost historically close.*"

After making my predictions, following the election was very exciting for me. I came to greatly admire Tim Russert's zeal and verve every Sunday morning on *Meet the Press*. George Stephanopoulos announced a "Democrat Dead Heat." Bingo… here we go. Another news channel labeled the standoff as "virtually tied." No one expected that type of race.

Then, the *exact words* I used in my predictions were used to describe the race. The first time I heard the words spoken aloud was on *Washington Week*, hosted by Gwen Ifil, aired on PBS February 15, 2008. Gloria Borger, the CNN political analyst announced, "*These folks are neck and neck.*" On Feb 19, 2008 on *ABC World News,* Charles Gibson repeated it. Several news stations described the race as *historically close.* I was months ahead of the news, just waiting for them to catch up.

Eventually, I created my own anonymous and experimental blog site (now dormant) to occasionally record my predictions.

Wednesday, March 10, 2011

Just an inkling, but that is often enough
I wrote in my blog:
"I am foreseeing a new wave of terror soon, and that means on the verge...a couple weeks at most. This is mostly going to be overseas incidents in the usual hot bed areas...like Pakistan/India or Bali. Always the same players...That's all I'm going to say for now, and that's all I have to say. Just a feeling. A dread that washes over me..."

Within a few days, the newscasters were talking about a "new wave of terrorism" in Pakistan. When it occurred, I was not surprised, but I got a slight case of the chills. This is my life. No one's watching. It is who I am. It makes up my consciousness. I can't control it or defy it, but at the very least I can speak about it.

Even when have I erred slightly in a prediction, I left it up on my blog for everyone to see. If I believed I could never be wrong, that would be a concern. That's not how this works.

I happened to watch on the end of a newscast in March of 2011 that a million sardines were packing in to the Bay area of California. I knew immediately why and was stunned that no one else could put two and two together. *An earthquake in the pacific was on the way.* I headlined my blog entry with the sardine event. I took it down a couple days later, embarrassed about its "fishiness" for fear of looking foolish—yes, even on an anonymous blog. Sometimes you cannot take yourself too seriously. Two days after deleting my post, an earthquake struck in Japan.

Before the young man attacked Sandy Hook Elementary School I had a dream of a man his age in a bathroom making bombs and I vividly saw one of the girls who was killed that day. She was in a dress of similar fashion and looked *exactly* the same, with a long blond braid. She was the spitting image of one of the girls who would later be repeatedly on the news and mourned in the hearts and minds of many people. What I wondered after this event occurred was why did I just see her face out of all the victims? Every dream is a little different. And sometimes they are spliced together.

For about two years before the attacks at the Boston Marathon I kept picking up the words "Boston market." I could only relate it to the restaurant I heard of and wondered why in the world it kept flashing into my consciousness. Like much of this, I wouldn't find out until later. Both of these events focused on New England.

In my world, things I need to know often fall into place, sometimes at the perfect time. I have come to recognize the mood. I have come to watch for the signs. You have to know where to look to be aware, and let life give you the signs. It's often said nothing happens by coincidence. A lot of people say, "no one can predict the future." But they haven't met me. The predictions described here are only a small fraction of all those I have made. The source seems never-ending. Though I have had my weak psychic days, I've made my case for precognition statistically greater than chance.

❦ 6 View From the Top

I think that as we make our way to adulthood, we keep inside us the people we were. Like Russian dolls, we can be taken apart until the smallest is revealed; each one holds dreams and desires that do not perish with time.

—Lucinda Franks

Have you ever noticed sometimes we are put in a place to help people? If you took a note pad with you and walked around, observing all the synchronistic coincidences around you, then you could connect the dots. This would put you in greater appreciation of what you can also draw from for information around you in your environment. Even on the hardest day, there will be some little sign meant to align you to keep on track in your own mission.

Right off of Brummett's Creek Road, in a beautiful valley where my grandmother once owned a cabin, I grew up joyfully playing and wandering the long creek searching for crinoids and crawdads with my cousins and friends. We lit sparklers on the porch every Fourth of July.

This was the place. We as kids got to listen to her wonderful life stories, which she loved to retell. Many were funny and a few were about the lessons she imparted to others in trying to promote the human condition. She was a journalist and publisher who had a knack for gently changing someone's point of view with intelligence, wit and charm. She earned her smarts. She was never without a hefty five-hundred page biography of some historical figure. And amazingly, she could remember everything she read. All of this helped put common problems of the world into perspective.

Later in life my parents bought some pristine acreage in the valley below my grandmother's home and built their home atop an enormous hill. For a time I got to stay in a bedroom perched so exquisitely high up it looked right out into the stars like a remote observatory. One day my stepfather was tractor-mowing in the field when suddenly the tractor stopped dead. When he got down to check things out he found a fawn bedded in the grass, previously completely out of his view. Nothing was wrong with the tractor. As soon as the deer moved it started right up again and had no further problems. I wondered what may have intervened to affect the laws of nature as we know them to be.

There comes a day when your family, hoping to encourage you to succeed, asks, "What do you *really* want to do with your life?" Now was my time to reach for the stars and pull them down into my life.

You can imagine the reaction when, again and again, I told them, "I want to be a professional psychic." From the looks on their faces, you'd think I said I wanted to run away with the circus or sell tickets to the moon!

Of course, their reaction stemmed from the fact that they were very skeptical about psychics. Finally, push came to shove. My mom and her husband brought up the subject one more time—here we go again!—and we had a truth-telling session.

I stuck to my guns, describing my abilities. Although I was

sick and tired of having to prove myself to everyone all the time, it came down to a demonstration. Seeing is believing, and I'd give them proof. I asked my stepfather to tell me the name of someone he knew that I did not, and I would give him personal details. He recited a name and instantly I received impressions.

I described the interior of this stranger's home, room by room as if I were there. Then I described his family: two daughters and their relative ages, his petite permed brunette wife, his personal hobbies and some of his illnesses. My step father's jaw dropped. My mom was just speechless—eerily quiet. I convinced them, but it was still something that they did not fully understand, appreciate or know how to accept. I was born psychic. I had used my abilities my whole life. But my mother was not a believer until then.

I continually requested that my family help me come up with ideas on how to make a living using my gift. It's what I wanted to do—what I just *had* to do with my life. I was just sitting on so much talent, so much promise. It was inconceivable to some, but nonetheless verifiable. My mom resolved to do what any caring mother would do to support me in this. "Okay already. Call the police. You need to find missing people." Next she reached for the local paper sitting on the table. "Here! Here is someone they're looking for—find him!"

I learned something very important from the way events were about to unfold. I needed to record my predictions in some notarized fashion. Otherwise, no one would back me up or give me credit for them. I couldn't just expect anyone to help me, least of all the authorities.

7 Most Wanted

I feel that my father's greatest legacy was the people he inspired to get involved in public service and their communities, to join the Peace Corps, to go into space. And really that generation transformed this country in civil rights, social justice, the economy and everything.

—Caroline Kennedy

My mother handed me a newspaper with a story about a most-wanted person, a terrorist. In retrospect it would have been a lot easier for me on down the road if the man were only an ax murderer.

The year was 1999. I envisioned the great psychic exercise this would be for me. I would tell authorities where he was, show them my psi-stuff, and maybe then someone would realize *exactly* what I can do and offer me the chance to assist in bringing home missing people and endangered children.

I was a dreamer.

Within the article, there was no mention of where they thought the fugitive would turn up or where he was suspected to be. There was just an Arabic name I didn't know how to pronounce—Ahmed—and a brief request for any information.

Paper in hand, I glided down the stairs to the phone. Before I could get there, I was given the knowledge I needed. My heart was open for it. No thought, no concentration required. I only had to listen in the precise way I had become accustomed to and accept it. It's hard to explain, but when I say *listen,* I don't suggest I actually hear someone speaking; it's cerebral. It's like a mental whisper (with leads from my heart).

The cities where he would be traveling flashed in my mind telepathically. The places came in clear and straight. I didn't even have to strain, as I sometimes do, for obfuscated details. I knew when I knew. Was it divine inspiration? I really don't know.

I hurriedly wrote down the place names. Sincerely, yet naively, I picked up the telephone and dialed the Indianapolis regional branch of the F.B.I. that the newspaper article had mentioned.

"Are you an F.B.I. *agent?*" I implored of the young man to whom I was connected. I wanted to make sure I got straight through to the top of the food chain with my vital information.

"I am an *Investigative Analyst,*" he replied. He sounded sure of himself. He gave me his "cryptonym," and I'll just call him Kevin.

I eagerly and succinctly shared a condensed version of my psi-bio. He listened silently, but keenly. To highlight the accuracy of my pre-cognitive dreams, I told him about my "fateful dream" involving planes striking the Twin Towers. Just to make it clear, I did not warn him that this dream was going to happen in the future, but included all the details of it as part of my past accurate psychic experiences. (After the bombing of the World Trade Center in 1993, I assumed this prophetic dream had already come to pass with certain relevancy to the scope and breadth of my abilities. I felt it proved that I have dreams of the future that come true, that it would help convince him of my veracity.)

I then told the Investigative Analyst what I knew about

the fugitive's future locations. I urged him to pass along the information immediately. "Based on past events," I told him, "I am sure this is going to come true, to happen as I see it. He will be there!"

The conversation was wholly one-sided and he did not encourage me to provide additional information. Reticent yet sincere, the analyst assured me he would pass the information on to his superior. I had no reason to believe otherwise.

❀ 8 A Hit

Man is only great when he acts from passion.
—Benjamin Disraeli

A few days later, I opened the newspaper and saw that I was right on target. At every location I had revealed to the F.B.I. analyst—the names of five specific U.S. airports—the fugitive was spotted and finally apprehended. I had psychically plotted his course of action.

I clutched the paper in my hands as proof of my multi-location prognostication. I again felt a renewed sense of appreciation for my gift. I knew I had to use it to help my country. My abilities were so strong; they just had to be meant for something big. I called the Investigative Analyst back. There was definitely tension about redialing the F.B.I.. I wondered why they didn't follow up with me.

I was informed the particular Analyst I spoke with would be out of the office for several months. My enthusiasm deflated. I was too timid to push the issue and explaining myself again to someone new. Still, I knew I would need credit for this prediction to help me convince other authorities of my abilities as I wanted to apply them to matters on a larger, more significant scale.

A straightforward, small-town kind of girl, I naively assumed I would encounter a two-way street. True, no one said they were open to working with psychics, nor were they particularly interested in seeing what I could offer. I was the only one talking and the line just went dead. Imagine, during this trying time in our history, how this would have been useful! And when I analyze myself, with my abilities, I feel one thing. I am on a spiritual mission. Maybe there is almost no one who can relate to that. But maybe there is higher purpose in the world, and a higher reason to what I can do after all.

9 Manifest Destiny

As you walk, you cut open and create that riverbed into which the stream of your descendants shall enter and flow.

—Nikos Kazantzakis

When I look back upon that day, it is with pain and awe. I may have been helpful in solving a mystery. Though it was nothing out of the ordinary for me, it still feels miraculous. I myself do not practice any religion. With that said, let me share with you part of my family's past. My Greek grandmother, Rebecca, has lived in California since I was born, and after I relocated to Indiana I had little time to spend with her.

Some people think we are all here for a reason. Given the background of my Greek heritage, you might agree my abilities are karmic payback.

My Greek grandmother, Rebecca, now known as Sister Seraphina, is currently a superior nun. The youngest of three sisters in a devout Orthodox Christian family, she lived in a village in Asia Minor at a time when Greece and Turkey were at war. One fateful day, Turkish attackers waited until all the men in her village were in the field, then ambushed and killed them as they worked. Next they swooped into the village and cut the throats of all the women and children. Her entire village was decimated.

Her mother, Evangelia ("good angel" in Greek) was praying when she was killed. Rebecca's two sisters, Destina and Joanne, were also killed. Rebecca, four years old, hid under a table and was the lone survivor.

Per Greek tradition, as her first granddaughter I am her namesake. She and I have always had a very deep bond. She is special. She has talked of visions of saints, as well as prophetic dreams that she writes down and sends to a monastery in Arizona. She does not know I am a psychic (my father is afraid to tell her) and my father did not tell me about my grandmother's dreams until I was in my late twenties. Her presence lights up a room like a candle in the darkness and her heart goes out to everyone. No matter the circumstances, she can make someone smile. You can feel love spill over from her kind eyes. She has a love for life and everyone.

I can also see the pain from her past when I look into her eyes. It's as if her soul briefly slipped out of place and the hurt is buried there. I cannot imagine living through her tragedy myself, but I believe she has overcome it through her faith and forgiveness. Later in her life, on a visit back to her village, the Turk (her neighbor) who had killed her family, asked for her forgiveness and she replied, "God has forgiven you."

Is it a coincidence that I foresee similar events like that one that destroyed her entire family? Perhaps it is more. Perhaps it paints an example of faith, mercy, and how God doles out justice in His perfect time. Perhaps it is destiny; perhaps my intuition stems from my ancestry. There are many possibilities. But they all point in one direction. Either you believe in God, or you don't. For the former, you likely believe in miracles. They come when you'd least expect them, in ways you'd never believe.

🌸 10 Prelude to Terror

For He shall give his angels charge over thee
to keep thee in all thy ways.

—Psalm 91:11

Sometimes you have to experience certain events to be able to appreciate something beyond that which we can explain. One of these for me included a year-long period when occasionally, from out of nowhere, tiny, cool droplets of water began to appear on my hands. This was a period of significant pain in my life. I was indoors when it happened—my hands were hanging down at my side. I kept ignoring it until I put two and two together—this was not happenstance—something must be trying to get into my system and perhaps cleanse or heal me.

I opened up to my father in California about it and he said rather matter-of-factly, "That is Holy Water." Like most of the extraordinary things in my life, I shared it with no one else.

Other times, the well would just burst. In mid-August 2001, I discussed my past of psychic encounters with a sympathetic nurse. Her exact response to me was, don't you think that sounds *a little strange* to call the F.B.I. about a psychic dream? (Well, not to me when they've all come true in the past.)

Just one more person to discount my "fateful dream." I reminded myself: who am I, after all? Even though I speak plainly and honestly from the heart, the world doesn't know what to think about people like me.

It's difficult enough to be given this information, to know that something bad is going to happen and be burdened with the urgent desire to help. When people refuse to listen or take me seriously, it makes the nightmare all the worse.

Fast forward to the end of August. I had a premonition of a terrible event, and wanted to call Condoleezza Rice, then National Security Advisor. I never before gave her any thought. After my previous experiences, I opted to keep it to myself.

Imagine for a moment what it would feel like to carry that weight, to have no one understand how serious you are or the gravity of what you are about to tell them. I can only try to reach out. Then someone has to meet me halfway, to help me from there.

Granted, with this premonition I did not sense *specifically* what would happen. I literally had no idea, only a perilous foreboding. I could only have advised them to remain alert—that I sensed imminent danger. Some need to hunker down. The timing of the warning would prove relevant.

🍂 11 New York Mourning

Faith is the strength by which a shattered world shall emerge into the light.

—Helen Keller

On the morning of September 11, 2001, I awoke, and, as part of my morning routine, turned on the radio for company. An announcer was talking about planes and buildings, but it took a while to sink in...My dream!

This was really happening.

My neighbor came over with tears rolling down her cheeks and took me to watch the events transpiring on her television. Like everyone else in America, my world had changed—my sense of security and freedom lost. Like everyone else in America, I grieved. But, unlike most everyone else, I wasn't surprised.

I didn't have the words, and barely do now, to explain how it felt to watch my very dream horrifically played out in real life. I had already seen the twisted metal, the burned-out buildings, the smoke, everything.

What upset me the most at that time was that in this world plagued by greed and complacency, that there are those who serve us by facing down pain, who work so hard for so little, who may be called to give their lives to help us in the most dangerous situations. That of those selfless heroes so many became casualties on that day felt like a deep wound in the very heart of this country. Our firefighters, our police—those are a *precious* few here among us.

Why was it so hard to get messages this important across? I am not in this for glory. I'm just here. I am *sure* I could not have been the only person in the world to have had this particular pre-cognitive dream. And it is agonizing for me that no one listened to or for that matter remembered any of us, that we had no one to tell. (I went back and reluctantly contacted some of the authority figures I could find with whom I shared my dream. They remembered me, but not the details of my premonition. Realistically speaking at that time they had no concern for strange psychics with dreams of large skyscrapers in Manhattan. All phone calls that go into the FBI about terrorism are supposed to be recorded, so something is around.)

With my neighbor in tears for fear she'd never live long enough to have a baby, and her father, a reserve officer of the law, sorrowfully pacing the hallway, I didn't bother speaking of my dream although I needed to. I yearned for someone who could relate to me. I was an outsider in every sense of the word. Besides, what good would it do now?

Later I told a parapsychology researcher about my dream and he said that it is more common to have a dream like that if you have a certain connection to the people or places. In my case it probably doesn't matter, but I later thought more about it. I worked for United Airlines once, which is how I got to visit Pearl Harbor. And I found out that my aunt through marriage, whose surname was York, comes from a multi-generational New York police family, none of whom I've met. The bedroom I had the fateful dream in was my cousin's (I was house-sitting). I'm told this cousin's former fiancée was in the Trade Center on 9/11/2001 and that she had wanted to go to the top of the building that morning but didn't want to pay the ticket price to ride the elevator and left before the attack. I'm sure there are probably more connections. Also, the numbers 9 and 11 had been haunting me for a long time, in personal identifiers, multiple addresses and later in phone numbers arbitrarily assigned to me. The future was something we all had to face. Some of the people affected by the future were familiar to me, maybe not the territory, but the conscious energies about to be affected. As I have since learned, no one is really ever separated.

I have to share my experience. I've kept it under wraps because my whole history has to be taken into account to see where I'm coming from. I'm still a little scared and precautious about sharing it. Also I think this is an "easy" prediction to have foreseen when understood in terms of the pre-cognitive experience as a whole because it is an event of infinite long-range consequences. But to gloat about it ad nauseam, as I've noticed a couple others do, is unsettling and distasteful. Secondly, I would not believe anyone who claims to have some supremacy over all others alone in having this prediction. I do believe in the existence of some higher power, though I do not feel it is my place to declare what precisely that means or how it works. However, my sentiment is that a power above us would inspire as many people as possible to foresee this type of tragic event to alert others. *That* is almighty. The truth is that this ability is about guidance in every sense of the word.

I immediately *knew*, by my intuition, that nothing else would happen to us in a big way for many years, but I was still as pensive, grieved, and as worried about attacks as everyone else. You can listen to your intuition, but you don't necessarily substitute it for common sense, especially after events like that.

The despair, the anger! Everyone wanted to find the man who was responsible for the attacks. It wasn't much like me, but I stayed out of the fray for several years.

❧ 12 A Patriotic Act

America will never be destroyed from the outside. If we falter and lose our freedoms, it will be because we destroyed ourselves.

—*Abraham Lincoln*

"Where is he?" I pondered, silently, in my heart. This is, after all, something I am good at. I am just as vulnerable to future attacks as any other American citizen. I am also just as patriotic. So I decided it was time I offered my talents in the highly-propagandized search around us.

Instantly, as if the information were poised and waiting for me, a location jolted into my brain: *Jalalabad*.

I felt that the world's most wanted fugitive, Osama bin Laden, would remain for the next few days in Jalalabad, *before changing locations later that week*. This was time-sensitive. I never heard of Jalalabad, but when I turned to an atlas, I found a city in Afghanistan by that exact name.

> *I asked Rebecca when my daughter's fiancé was going to be back from Iraq. She told me it would be the middle of January 2011. He flew in on the afternoon of the 14th of January.*
>
> —*Sue Jordan*

From past experience, I knew when dire information leapt

into my brain spontaneously like an inspiration— without me having to agonizingly ply my own inner guidance—that it was good psi-intel.

There was, at the time, an informant program called the "Rewards for Justice Program," to help capture the alleged mastermind behind the September 11th attacks. Though my motivation was not monetary at all—I just desperately wanted to prevent future attacks—I did what every other safety-conscious American would do who had "pertinent" information. I rushed to tell the government what I knew.

I went to the website and was about to enter the data electronically. Eerily, a contradictory warning in my mind admonished me: *Don't!*

Ridiculous, I thought. *I am not afraid.* I had no reason to distrust or fear the government of my own country. I'm a loyal American. My government is righteous and fair. They would know just what to do with this information and use it to protect us. What's to fear, when the cause is just?

By this time I should have learned to heed my intuition.

Many psychics have reported being under surveillance after going public with warnings related to national security. Having their privacy invaded often intimidates psychics from speaking up.

Suffice to say, after I reported my intuition, they never bothered asking me any questions, which would have been fair. The most I'm going to reveal for these purposes is that I have, at various times, been followed by "professional" men in dark sunglasses.

Remember that old adage about shooting the messenger? Consider the following, quoting a retired special agent of the F.B.I., from an article in the magazine *Life: Unsolved Mysteries* by Robert O'Brian:

"If somebody claiming to be psychic produced information they

couldn't have known, like the location of a body, an experienced investigator would immediately consider that person a suspect in the crime."

This is the pervasive mentality. And let's face it, for all practical purposes, I did locate someone, in a location that I not only couldn't know, but had never even heard of. A year before he was eventually caught, I knew Pakistan should be the rendezvous point. By then I had quit trying to point out where fugitives were hiding. Anyhow, I have a voice that tends to get droned out.

As a psychic in tune with national security I would have liked to have been a part of your safety net. My only regret is that my abilities couldn't be put to use to help you without subjecting myself to possible repercussions.

13 Psychic Shazaam Network

The way is not in the sky. It's in the heart.
—*Buddha*

I was still not working as a psychic. I didn't have money to rent an office or advertise my services. A majority of the time I couldn't even *give* my readings away! (If I did, people discounted my value.)

I was motivated, but I needed professional help before starting up a business. I went to a volunteer-based business mentoring service. Though attentive, kind and professional, their small business counselors basically determined "there is no business model to use" for psychics, and recommended I re-focus my efforts on becoming a magician because magicians draw big, happy crowds. I am NOT a magician (magicians use illusion—fakery, although skillfully). Also, I am uncomfortable performing before a crowd.

So, with big future events jumping into my mind on a steady basis, I searched for one person who might be able to help me begin working professionally as a psychic. I approached other working psychics, calling and sending polite e-mails, but none ever showed up to meet me or return my calls. Not even the ones that claimed "unconditional love" in the bylines of their advertisements. The more "Hollywood" they were, the less caring they were.

I decided to work on a psychic phone hotline. Their advertisements promised I'd make twenty dollars an hour working from home! I thought it strange that the majority of these outfits mainly want to know if you had experience using software, but I pursued the job anyway.

My test examiner's requirements were stringent: she could neither ask nor say *anything*, and I was not allowed to ask anything, but simply divulge psychic input about her. I did tell her I needed her to say her name at least, in order to get some vibrations. She gave me only her first name.

I provided some personal details about her, and picked up on two medical conditions, one of which was pretty out of the ordinary. She kind of gasped and verified that I was right. She told me I would do really well, plus I had such a "lovely voice." I was hired.

My first day arrived. Here we go! I picked up the phone, entered my little code number when prompted, and instantly all the psychic addicts were chomping at the bit to talk to the brand new psychic. As soon as one call ended, the phone rang the very next second.

The first client was, surprisingly, a man. He was yelling about his girlfriend losing interest in him and didn't particularly want any psychic feedback.

The next caller was a very distant and demanding woman who wanted to know if her boyfriend was cheating on her. I confirmed what she already suspected. Then she wanted to find out, in case the other woman got pregnant, what their offspring would look like—and more specifically, what color their kids' hair would be.

It went on like that for hours, until the callers grew tired of waiting for their chance to talk. Eventually the phone stopped ringing. After that spurt, there were only a few phone calls each shift.

I wasn't told what to expect. Most of those who called were abusive, ingrates or sexual deviants. I didn't want to sit inside my home twiddling my fingers, waiting for the phone to ring, so I tried seeing how far my cordless phone reception would go, dashing back inside my home when I received a call. I can't tell you how many times I had to tell a caller that their ex was not coming back to them and they'd hang up on me. Clearly if I were in this for the money it was not going to be lucrative for me. I just wanted to work using my gift.

This was my first official job as a psychic, and hotline or not, I was still working with clients over the phone and took it seriously. I was extremely surprised at my ability to pick up precisely on health conditions, though people did not typically have serious medical concerns. But more often than not, callers weren't looking for medical help—they simply wanted to know the date of their next sexual encounter. Many callers were cheating on their mates and desperately afraid that their mates were also cheating on them. The nerve!

> *Because I am so far away I opted for a phone consultation. Again I was pleased with the level of correctness even at a distance. From health to relationships, the information I have received from you has been right on whether by phone or in person. ...You are a talented and gifted woman who sees, hears and feels the energy around you and others without an agenda. Your genuine caring attitude is one of generosity and concern for the well-being of your client as each time we have met, you have given more time and more help than were originally solicited. I appreciate that we have met and feel it is one more synchronized piece of the puzzle that is my life.*
>
> *—D.*

I was grateful when I was able to use my abilities to help someone overcome pain of any sort. Selena, agonized by a breakup with her boyfriend, couldn't let him go even though he was in a new relationship. She winced and begged relentlessly, pleading with me to give her for a sign from the Heavens—when will he call? I told her the truth as I always did. He wouldn't call her—she was more likely to call him. But I stressed—did she want him to? I described his personality faults, encouraged her to move on and set her sights higher. I made her think more realistically.

She found my words inspiring. Though discouraged he wasn't going to come back to her, she seemed pleased, if not surprised. "All the *other* psychics on your hotline have been telling me *I just need to wait and be patient and he'll come back to me*," she declared. For us both it was like suddenly a ball dropped on my blind faith in people who claim to be psychic. This cemented my suspicions about the lack of authenticity of some of the other psychics on the hotline. Despite that I know there are some real psychics working on hotlines. You just never know what you're going to get.

A caller named Jade had brief, no-nonsense questions, but I was concerned when she became a regular. I did not want to be the source of her dependency. In fact I found it demoralizing when she called me again the next week. I wanted her to feel strong enough to rely on her own judgment for making life-changing decisions, not a psychic on a phone line with a pseudonym whom she had never even met.

My fears about her were well-founded. One night she revealed that she just received a personal letter from a preacher she watches on television. The letter read that the "good Lord" had informed him that her single-parent household was going to receive between "$3,500 and $45,000 on October 17." Hallelujah!

I was stunned and angry. She trusted him as a spiritual advisor and said she had been sending in money to "help them out." I felt very sorry for her and tried to let her down easy. It really upset me that someone would take advantage of others that way using God's name. I sent her an e-mail in all caps that told her to stop and think critically before she acts. The hotline management told us to email people and even gave us pre-prepared suggestions. These messages were intended to get people to keep calling back. The suggested communiques read like moronic lines from soap opera written by someone with a third-grade education. I wouldn't stoop that low. We also were sent a directive that we should to try to keep people on the line longer—at least twenty minutes. Again, I refused. I'm not taking advantage of people.

A refreshing break from the monotonous "love readings" was Leopold. A devotee of the *Coast to Coast* AM radio program, he claimed to be experiencing all of the different types of phenomena discussed on the late night Pandora's-grab-box kind of show. I listened to his tales of spacecraft waiting for him, abduction theories and aliens taking over the planet. It was all very complicated and hard to keep up with. It involved Atlantis, the antennae in his backyard, his crystals and the medallions that he makes special-order as directed by the extra-terrestrials asking him to be their commander/king, once he finds a female who is "queen material." (He's a Gemini, in case you're interested.)

The very last call I accepted on the hotline happened to be from Leopold. A week earlier he had called to ask if his daughter sneaked off with his car while he was asleep. Tonight he wanted to know how to woo an actress from a hit television show about superheroes. He paid my employers $120.00 for that last call. Though my cut was supposed to be 7%, I never received my last paycheck. My paychecks were never more than thirty dollars anyhow. The great wizard behind the curtain pulling the strings— located in Las Vegas, Nevada, of course—has little consideration once the ruby slippers have left the building.

14 Up Goes My Shingle

We make a living by what we get, but we make a life by what we give.
—Winston Churchill

With my artist mother's help, I finally began a business of my own, the two of us sharing a little space in a seasonal-tourist town.

Initially she spotted a for-rent ad in the paper for a high-visibility, historic building occupied by varied businesses: a candy shop, a kitchenware store, some yoga studios and a few art studios. She inquired only to receive an abrupt call from the owner who told her that "his brother" refused to have a psychic in the building. It didn't really bother me. Hailing from the West Coast, I was aware of the more conservative folks in Indiana.

Rebecca told me things that I had already said or thought (sometimes VERBATIM!), and confirmed my feelings that a relationship was wrong for me. Sometimes, it's our fears that stop us from realizing what we already know. And it's people like Rebecca that can guide us through these times in our lives. She truly has been a gift in my life and I credit her for finally waking up a part of me I'd buried a long, long time ago. The ears long to hear what the heart already knows, and Rebecca makes a caring and gentle messenger.

— Rachel

Which is worse: a psychic reading that provides preventive measures by detecting a tumor you can't see, or peanut butter fudge sold by the pound that causes cavities, childhood obesity, hyperactivity and type II diabetes? It's a matter of perspective, I guess.

When we did find a suitable suite to rent from a landlord who actually appreciated my profession, we signed on the dotted line. My mother had one spacious room for painting, showing and selling her artwork and I occupied a large pyramidal storage room with a window.

At once I began drawing in really good clients, from nurses to teachers to doctors. Turns out not every professional in this world is a skeptic. I prematurely expected to mostly see mostly hippie types. No, they didn't want me; they stuck with the local palm reader. I did have one teenage girl who insisted she was a vampire, but otherwise appeared normal. I'm sure she was influenced by a very popular series of movies at the time.

What are readings with me like? I do not begin with a jive prayer, upturn my hands to the sun or do anything else that needlessly takes up time. I don't drown the room with singing bowls music and I avoid *anything* that would bother me. (I don't mean to disparage other psychics, just to describe what works for me.) It requires intense focus, tranquility and major quiet. I simply sharpen my senses and steady my focus toward deliberately helping the person sitting in front of me through my extra receptivity. All that's required is that I block out my own feelings to tap into theirs. I am in a state of absorption.

I do begin by holding onto a personal object, which can be indicative of how well I will be able to read my client's energy. Psychometry—or reading through an object—is one of my specialties. Everything around us is made up of energy—people pulsate with it, places and ob-jects hold it. This unseen energy flows around us, bristling with information that can be read by those who have the ability to feel it. If I don't pick up much of anything from holding the object it feels cold and means the client's energy is blocked from my reception. And there is nothing I can do to change that.

A photograph is very much like a fingerprint to a psychic sleuth, and it's never static. It's as if it contains ridges or rivulets of data. Not only does a picture tell a thousand words, it betrays our secrets. It's a curious fact to me that some tribes supposedly believe a picture can steal one's soul.

> Rebecca has been instrumental in my life since my first reading with her last year.
>
> My first visit with her, I gave her a ring I was wearing, which had belonged to an ex. The energy she received from that ring gave her a vision of a trip to Hot Springs in my future, within the next 6 months. I knew that seemed unlikely as I knew of only one Hot Springs and that was in Arkansas. However, within 4 months of my reading, my ex went to Hot Springs in NC with someone.
>
> My readings with Rebecca help guide me in my journey through life and have been more helpful than any therapist I have seen. I am so thankful to have her as a resource in my life!
>
> —Theresa S.

Just starting out, I charged very little and worked with the basics I had seen success with in the past, working my way up the ladder.

When handed a photo of a young boy with perfect, straight white teeth I remarked, "Even though it looks like his teeth are healthy, I sense he has a pain issue with them." It turned out he has a very painful problem with the enamel on his teeth. From looking at his typical family photograph I picked up on the fact that the mother had been in a motorcycle accident, her spine and right leg were hurt, she suffers from depression and has trouble with her uterus. There was nothing from their lifestyle or attire to even faintly suggest the woman would get on the back of a bike. I just go with the flow—of energy. I have been able to deduce as much information about someone—both physically and emotionally—from their photo as I am from reading them in person.

At no time in the session do I ask for any kind of descriptive information from my client, such as date of birth. It is my job to supply all the hidden details without any help. At the outset of a reading, straight off the bat, I want to give people information they can confirm so they know that I am for real and we both can relax from there.

Every day, I hear heartbreaking stories. Much of my role is therapeutic. People need someone who can really get a feel for what is going on in their lives and how it has affected them. They need someone to point out their ability to overcome loss and reclaim their lives. Many of my clients begin crying from relief as I tell them what I empathically feel they are experiencing.

As my clairvoyance improved, I began to intimately sense what was going on inside and out of a person's body, even when that person wasn't physically in the room. It always tickles me when, for instance, a mother asks about her son, but says, "Maybe you can't read him—he's three thousand miles away." None of that matters, but I think it's very understandable that they feel there would be those types of restrictions. It's the same with phone readings; distance doesn't apply. By minutely altering my senses, I can focus on a subject not present and I can duplicate, so to speak, his energy, internalize it, and report my feelings.

I began a reading for a female truck driver. She didn't seem like the sympathetic type, so when I psychically intuited she was transporting hazardous and toxic materials, she lifted her reserve and I was glad I got it right. I asked for her partner's name, only. This is simply how I trained myself. I use the name to "dial-up" their energy. I have to consciously make a break from the client in front of me to do this and that's where the greatest effort is required. I was able to intuit the fact that her partner in Alaska had been dealing with cancerous growths on her hand.

Many people wonder how I know I'm right about my feelings. When people experiment with their own intuitions, being absolutely certain of one's conclusions is always a stumbling block. For me I feel a certain heaviness on the tip of my tongue, light pressure tugging at my heart and sure clarity of my mental senses. I just know. My faith in this process is resolute and I am working to help others. It's far removed from the energetically abstinent practice of say, selecting lottery numbers. That's not what intuition is geared for. There is something alive at stake. There is virtue in the undertaking.

When I have a bad head cold I am unable to read at all—whatsoever. Not because I feel bad or for lack of trying. When my head is blocked up I actually lose my ability to tune into the object/subject in question. Perhaps it interferes with the saccule, a pea sized organ in the inner ear most often associated with balance, which is also sensitive to ultrasonic sound.

About half my clients desire mediumship readings.

A very bright client who was adopted and now works at Fort Knox wanted some information on her birth father, about whom she knew next to nothing. While concentrating on seeking his identity and whereabouts, I soon felt myself connecting to him—he had passed on. I sensed that fact in my mind while I felt his energy in the room. I told her everything I could pick up about him. He was a writer, I explained. I told her that he wrote a poem expressly for her.

"Yes," she burst out, crying joyfully, "I have a poem he left for me." That was all she had of him. It was very touching. She had never met him until that day, essentially re-connecting in the only way possible. I helped her put the pieces of her past together and it seemed like she finally knew herself again.

Some parents refuse to ever stop grieving, especially if their child died unexpectedly. They hold it against themselves. What happens in a session with a parent who has lost a child is beyond my comprehension. The communication comes directly through my heart, expressly intended to help heal someone in great pain. It's an enormous gift, an act of love, like I'm literally joining two hearts together in prayer. I know there is nothing else that can touch a parent who has experienced this kind of grief; they've told me. When I work with the bereaved by sharing communication from a loved one in the beyond, I see layer after layer of heartache peel away, replaced by tear-releasing comfort.

I counseled a sister whose young brother died when he wrecked his vehicle. They were very close. She was unsure whether or not it was suicide due to some of his past erratic behavior. If it had been suicide she couldn't forgive herself for not having tried harder to prevent it.

Once I connected with his spirit, I was able to provide her details that gave her great relief—he was not trying to end his life. I told her the color and make of his vehicle; that the seat belt had been torn *before* the accident; that he was just about to take classes at a community college to move ahead with his life; that he had a new baby, and plans for an upcoming trip. Also, for some reason his cousin's name, "Sabrina," came up.

The woman acknowledged everything. "You just gave me chills," she said, when I described the issue with the seat belt. They discovered it had been torn when the accident was investigated. And although the brother also explained via telepathy to me that he was having trouble sleeping and drinking too many energy drinks, he hadn't intentionally overdosed or wrecked his car.

She left a different person. It was amazing to see the transformation. Those who lose a family member to an undetermined cause of death seem to have a great need for closure. This woman received insight about her brother so meaningful to her that nothing else could have filled the void, which put her at peace. Though she entered stiff, sorrowful and in pain, she left her real self again, with hope and a sense of renewal.

I began to find it exceptionally draining to focus on mediumistic readings. The deceased person's energy overtakes me. The spirits have a tendency to "camp out" in my space after a session and I can only put up with so many sensations all the time.

One reading zapped my energy so entirely I had to lie down for an hour until I recovered. Ten questions from a woman for her departed husband, mother, and Aunt Bernice and my mind bucked in revolt.

Sometimes a connection is easy; other times it's strained. It's nothing I can guarantee will happen for someone. Sometimes I get a sharp pain that accumulates like a subcutaneous welt just over my left eyebrow when someone is trying really hard to connect with me from beyond. It's different with every client; this part of a psychic reading is as unexpected as it gets. It's up to the departed whether they come through— and not all will. I do not promote myself this way. If it happens, it happens.

Some clients require some proof before they can get comfortable in a reading. Some believe in psychics, but aren't sure *I* am one. Interestingly, they ignore the fact that I tell them I have a guarantee of authenticity, meaning if I don't make a psychic connection I don't accept payment and then only at the close of the session. There have been a couple times I'm so worn out I forget to get payment.

One woman came in and asked me outright, "Can you tell what I do?" I responded by identifying not only the three-part occupational title, but the actual name of the business. When I first started out I was hot, hot, hot. I don't expect that to happen all the time— sometimes I just get super-stellar hits with my ESP. It is by nature, wild.

Once I lock into someone's energy, I begin firing off information, not only about themselves, but those connected to them as well. I can describe an individual's personality and his mind-set—all those little idiosyncrasies so individual to us.

The majority of men who seek me out do their research online before approaching me. These clients tend to be deft, savvy and know about educated risks. They want to stay in control, gain a better perspective and continue on course to achievement. They separate this work from luck. Relying on luck does not give a proactive advantage. Seeing all sides of the equation, however, can.

Here is an email exchange with my client Dave who is a pilot from North Carolina:

I was scheduling his appointment when I wrote, "I had an interesting dream about you and your family last night... Also, before I forget, a name of an airport keeps coming up: "McCarren."

He emailed me back: "Very strange . . . I'm going on a trip tomorrow, to McCarran airport in Las Vegas! I'm flying a guy there for the night and then back to Florida the next day." You are right on again, as always."

Men can also be more skeptical and many do not relish asking questions. One man came in and asked me if he had any children. I sat silently in my rocking chair, focusing, until I picked up the information. Confidently I replied, "Yes, you had one son, but he was stillborn."

He confirmed calmly, "Yes—that was good." Then he followed

with "Hope you didn't think I was testing you." I didn't necessarily think that, but people have tried throwing those types of things at me in the beginning of a session, after which they seem to feel badly about doubting me. No, I'm not a fake—that's why I can offer a guarantee.

> *The real deal! Rebecca's gift allows her to provide comfort and knowing when life shows you seemingly impossible situations.*
>
> —Dave

A husband and wife came down from the big city for one-hour sessions each. This was a red-letter day for me, since I was new in business and was often doing fifteen-minute sessions for tourists who happened by. The husband was first in line. Straight off the bat he asked me, "Will my wife have another child?"

"No, I don't think that's physically possible," I answered, straightforwardly.

He replied, "I see—well, she's had a hysterectomy," he grinned. I guess I was right, then. (I had envisioned a blank in her uterus.) He was very silent for a few moments before mustering up the nerve to ask me his next question.

Although I don't like to be tested, I guess I understand it. All of these stories you are reading about so far are from people who were complete strangers. They don't know me and I don't know them. I try to briefly explain what I offer, which is no easy task because I am not a salesperson. From there on the decision to see me rests in their hearts. Time and again I have dealt with the humiliation of rejection, but if they are comfortable, they will select me. The proof will inevitably be in their reading. Often, a group of friends appears together to inquire about my services.

"Gina, are you gonna go?"

"Yeah, I'm in."

"Sis—are you gonna go?"

"Yes!"

"Tina??"

"I don't know—no!"

I only read for one person at a time. The group hurriedly makes way as my first client slips off her shoes and begins to become "entranced." The others wait outside, huddled, whispering amongst themselves. As the first person exits my office, the rest of the flock is waiting on pins and needles to hear what I said—how it went. What always follows is a line-by-line breakdown. The group huddles like a team on a scrimmage line around my client who is still wiping away tears from her cheeks, elated for the clarity, detail and emotional release it brings. Soon, the next one makes a bee-line to my door, thinking, *I hope she can read me that well, too.*

As each member of the group takes their turn, the conversational buzz begins to mellow. Another person leaves my office and I take a deep breath, waiting for the next. Here's the funny part. Not everyone believes in psychics, but they tend to adjust their opinion once they've heard the feedback from *all* their combined friends and family. First-hand accounts are persuasive but all the same, it can take hours to wash away that uncertainty.

More often than not, by the end of the day, that lone holdout, the one who didn't want a reading or didn't originally "believe in any of this" shows up to ask if I have any time left— even imploring me for a reading. Some of these holdovers may still be a little psychically reserved, but they've been softened by hearing from their family and friends how I helped them.

Such was the case with Paula. When she sat down, I thought *no!* This can't work. She had the countenance of chiseled rock, unyielding with a pained look of horror on her face from allowing herself to be at my mercy for a reading.

"Tell me about my husband's health," she asked point-blank.

I shifted my concentration to him, to his energy. I began to get impulses in my mind. "He had a problem with his liver when he was younger but that has cleared up now."

"Yes, he had hepatitis in his childhood," she verified aloud. As I gave her the rundown, her eyebrows lifted and stretched and her shoulders finally sank with ease. A wowed expression passed over her face.

"He is nice and kind," I added, switching gears.

"Well, I told all my sisters if you didn't say *that* I was going to leave!" It's rare that I can give a wife such a straightforward compliment about her relationship with her husband. Next she wanted to me tell her about her son's career.

"He is going to be in law enforcement," I replied.

"Yes!" She practically stood up at attention and exclaimed "He is majoring in criminal justice."

Paula confessed that her earlier resistance to me had stemmed from a kind of religious concern, but I had opened her eyes. It took careful deliberation for her to trust in me. She then opened up to me and admitted, "You know, my son always told me if someone did have this gift it would be used for something good."

That is what I have been trying to say all along!

One afternoon I had to read a woman who was part of the group gathered to pry my psychic tool chest. Looking at her I could tell her visit was paradoxical at best. She would not be plausibly engaged in these effective applications to her life.

"How old am I?" she fronted. (Ugh). Thankfully I nailed it. Once I told her that key number she got all she was after—to determine whether or not I was a real psychic or if her assorted family members were all "off their rockers" in seeing me. I guess with her there was no way you could tell by looking. She fell into that 20-year gap, where either good genes, rest and clean living helped you, or the opposite ripened your surface like a prune.

I was not in a financial position to turn away those who came to me with a hesitant attitude, or who were reluctantly dragged in by a friend or spouse. I had to accept everyone even though it turned my stomach sour. Though some of the skeptics would come to believe, others' doubting energy was so negative that the currents prevented me from reading them. It was like playing tug of war with Hulk Hogan— game over before it began. Contrasting energies are formed when there is no meeting of the minds.

Three women came into my office. None of them were smiling. I knew they were on the fence—that was okay, but I sensed one of them really needed a reading and I told her so. This scared her. She was hesitant, but at that time I charged very little, so, nervous and stiff, she sat down and asked about her daughter's life and I tuned in.

I felt her daughter could work but she doesn't really want to. I looked into my client's sallow, confused face and declared that there is a condition with her daughter's heart.

She responded "Well, she's applied for disability, but I don't know if she's ever going to get it. The doctor said she has a heart condition, but I do not think so—anymore..." Clearly she wasn't ready or willing to accept what I was telling her. Her doubts were holding back my ability to read her. Working with her I felt like I was all thumbs. I didn't charge her for the reading; I want people to leave happy.

From this experience I decided that it's best at the first sign someone is egged on by friends, but hems and haws with an "I don't know...I don't think I want to," to not proceed with a reading. It is too much work for me if they don't care about or believe in psychic energy. Usually, after the reading is over, they still feel the same way, even after I've proven my accuracy. *It just didn't happen*—they block the truth, fighting it with their sleeves rolled up.

There have been exceptions. A professor from Purdue University—who claimed to be one of the top three in his field—came to see me with his fashion-forward, retired psychologist girlfriend. He sat down on my little sofa and I proceeded to go over what to expect in the reading. He egotistically passed back my informational guide, denouncing it brutally with, "I'm not expecting *anything!*"

As the reading progressed, however, he kept extending his time. As happens with many men, for some reason more so than with women, he became totally transfixed. His time was up, but he was anchored to the chair, spellbound and stunned like a deer in headlights. The session was well over the hour. I had to move my chair back, get up and motion toward the exit.

He told me he never believed in psychics. He had never had a reason to. He recounted going to see a psychic located in Roswell (seriously), but that she couldn't read him. He said my accuracy was incredible. I described everything happening with his brothers and at work to a "t". He was extremely impressed and went on and on, asking when he could return. Never let a tough exterior fool you.

At the end of one session a husband from a mom-and-pop paranormal investigative crew asked me if marijuana or other drugs can create the lush mental environment required to receive psychic impressions. I flat out advised him no. In fact I thought it odd he would ask.

Incensed that his private research had misled him, he actually protested. "My wife would disagree with you." All I know is that stimulants are not part of what I do. I need and want to be in command of my senses. That's because pure psychic ability is a reality. Clairecognizance is just that—you are cognizant.

I have asked people why they are so scared of psychics. I often hear people say they are afraid to hear that someone will die. I will not predict death.

The body provides for survival and can be very crafty when it comes to issuing defense measures. It's the reverse of letting down your guard. Don't underestimate it. It works for you in the background—you don't always consciously work for it. The brain is a meter and we are a receptor. The brain slips easily, or transgresses into different levels of consciousness. There are individual flashes of intuition versus the longing for knowledge. Longing is the conscious effort to exercise that muscle. Warnings take on an autonomous quality.

Sometimes it's not just you that can be saved. A new shopkeeper shared her husband's story. While never recollecting a psychic "rush" of information before, one rainy evening while driving, he suddenly had a vision of a bicyclist veering in front of his car. A few minutes later it happened and he barely avoided it. When they met me, they told me that experience was the reason they believed in psychic abilities. In fact, psychic abilities work hand in hand with our most commonly appreciated senses. It doesn't negate the five senses; it boosts them, reinforcing your defenses.

Early on in my readings, I began picking up the names of medical diagnoses, even when I had no idea what the words meant. I would cautiously say something, and, sure enough, the client would confirm it. I was amazed that I was correctly receiving the names of clients' medical conditions.

A slender woman walked in and I held onto her ring for a few moments. The first thing I said was, "Your blood sugar is high."

> *We have four house cats that never go outside, but one evening, Bunny, the youngest, turned up missing. We searched all over the house and outside, but could not find Bunny. And after two more days of frantic searching, there was still no sign of Bunny. At that point we contacted Rebecca.*
>
> *The only information we could give Rebecca was Bunny's name; we had no photo of her. We were not even sure what day she disappeared. Rebecca said that Bunny was-at that moment-not that far away near a pink house with a billboard type of sign to her left and a very small bridge to her right. She was in good condition and would most likely return home during the night five days from then.*
>
> *We found a pink house and that type of sign about a block away from home, but did not find Bunny. We kept looking day after day and still did not find her-until on exactly the fifth night-there she was- sitting outside in the backyard, a little thinner but in good shape and home as predicted.*
>
> *That reading really took the edge off things when we heard about it and then became stratospheric when your prediction came true.*
>
> —M. A. Jones

To my surprise, she immediately pulled out and unzipped her diabetes test kit, pricked herself, and confirmed, "Yes it is." She corrected the situation forthright.

I do not diagnose specific diseases, only symptoms. But I've learned that the medical information I receive is valuable to my clients, and that I should not censor it. Sometimes I have even picked up on the medication they are taking, obscure names I've never heard before. For their protection, at the start of a session I always let clients know that I have no medical expertise and they should check with a doctor about anything I sense. They get it. They don't come to me for a diagnosis. They tend to come to me for impressions of their health, or to see if they are missing or overlooking something in their or their families' overall health.

Clients often ask for information about their pets and many are taken aback by my accuracy. Please don't confuse this with Doctor Doolittle. As someone who is sensitive to feelings, I don't pick up things animals are *saying*, but rather their experiences, which transcend language.

For me, reading animals is just like reading people. I detect feelings and emotions that are universal and trans-species. In fact, it's easier because there's no stubbornness to get in the way like it does with the human psyche. When I first tried to read pets I was absolutely certain I needed a picture from which to pick up their energy. Over time, through faith and experimentation, the training wheels loosened and photos became redundant and unnecessary (just as it did for people readings).

An animal's brain may be less evolved than our own, but it's still a brain. It emits signals. Goodness knows animals pick up on our feelings—even when we're apart—very effectively.

Animals are a part of the family and have very meaningful relationships with their humans. Surprisingly, what I pick up the most about pets is that they care about *your* feelings. These are their worries: *Is my guardian okay? Does she love and accept me? Will we move? What have those neighbor's teenage sons been up to in their garage?* In general, their concerns are not for themselves. Most of all, animals want to make things right. They are perfect and flawless in that way.

I enjoy reading animals as it helps unravel complicated behavioral problems they may be exhibiting. It really can improve your relationship with your pet as well as the pet's wellness. Animals know when you are upset with them for their behavior, but they don't understand why you are upset. For example, their instincts tell them to do something, like void to mark territory.

Our decorating and cleaning bill is not ingrained in their behavioral compass; furniture holds no value to them. Because they live in your house, they naturally think they own it, too. Unto themselves they are not a pet.

The highest percentage of pet questions I receive concerns man's best friend. I've read all kinds of dogs, but also horses (actually the easiest for me), cats galore, a feisty ferret and a bird on the lam.

One young woman came in for a reading because she missed her departed chicken, *Chi Chi*. She wanted to make sure that she had done everything she could for him in this life and that he was okay on the other side.

Although I didn't expect it, I connected very easily to her chicken's soul, sensed he had respiratory problems in life and was a rather smart animal. There is no animal too low on the food chain to be "valued" in the afterlife. I believe if something has a heartbeat it has a consciousness.

Getting a reading from a good psychic will not solve everything, nor will a good psychic see everything. But a good psychic will find your strengths and encourage you to overcome your weaknesses, including those you don't know you have. It's a nice way to give your soul a "tune up."

For many people who let the pain of their pasts rule their lives, there is a lesson to be learned from the tragedies the following two clients have struggled to overcome. A grandmother was raising her granddaughter because her daughter was a crack addict who had syphilis, became pregnant, and gave her up her baby. Upon birth the newborn was covered with large open sores on her vagina (the STD) and had four holes in her heart (corroded by drugs) that had to be operated on immediately. Two years had passed from that day and this extremely drained, caring and pensive grandmother wanted to know if the baby's next cardio-thoracic round of surgery was going to be a success. Imagine what she had to take on. This should make you realize how lucky you are.

A kind and timid young woman came in to see me. As a *child*, she had been raped by her biological father then her stepfather throughout her youth. By the session's end I could visibly see the effect the session had on her. I sensed I had given her something she could not see on her own. A serene, glow emanated from her cheeks and eyes. Unexpectedly, she hugged me as if she'd known me forever. I was amazed at the strength of her heart to overcome that adversity.

Many people have struggled to keep up with the current of life's events. You will never know what the people you come across have lived through, mostly women, so please treat each other kindly. Be nice. And while you're at it, let go of what you're harboring; it could be worse. Not everything is ever as bleak as it seems.

As part of my readings, I urge clients to ask me the question: "Is there anything I need to know to protect myself?" This allows me to focus my mind on identifying trouble spots— particular things wrong inside their homes, situations in their workplaces and neighborhoods, vulnerabilities with their vehicles, and more rarely, dangerous peoples' intentions. If there is a problem, I'm likely to find it through a process that mimics remote viewing, all springing forth from that one question.

Sometimes, the problem is something they are aware of and have been putting off fixing. "I have someone coming next week to fix that," a client has often replied. I don't just identify the problem, I like to explain its root source, often improving upon information they already have.

One woman asked me about her job. I mentally fished around her workplace and notified her, "You have had a gas leak there. I see this building crumbling down." She concurred, explaining the leak was methane from a nearby sewer and the building was scheduled for demolition. Turns out she was a ballerina working in an old gym.

I have enabled my mind to work with precision. When it comes to their welfare, my clients know I am sincere because I empower them to see for themselves and to be safer.

I practiced the art of "remote viewing" for years on my own. I like to that term because it seems so much more descriptive of the more scientific process of exploring all the intricate nooks and crannies of an environment. It's like a blueprint forms in my mind.

Early on, I used computer-model exercises, where I stared at a blank screen and enabled my mind to pierce into a futuristic stratosphere. Though I found it overwhelmingly draining, the practice does enhance clairvoyance. Before going to work as a psychic I partook of the exercises offered by the website www. gotpsi.com. On this website there are tests that extend beyond Zener symbol cards. I found it to be an engaging outlet for my ESP, which needed its own little playground to run around in— hop, skip, jump and develop.

Clairvoyance is like a bridge between the mind's and the eye's perception. You must be eager to do this work—to go beyond hitting the snooze button in your mind. I learned the ins-and-outs of a deeper, inner sense—a vision that comes from within. I compare it to an infant learning a new language. There is a developmental process. Just like exercising any muscle, the more I worked at it, the more I improved—heightening old abilities and developing new manifestations of psychic energy. Believe me, it can stretch. This is especially the case with clairvoyance, which is honed over time.

When I was young my favorite television program was

Rebecca Bartlett

Unsolved Mysteries. I found myself exclaiming how the victim died before the story began. I just knew.

Sadly, it's always been disheartening for me to learn of the summation of a long jury trial resulting in the conviction of an innocent, where I sense differently. The uses of a psychic with crystal-clear vision include not only to curtail pain, but to save lives and to bring justice to a system so parched. We take the negative and try to restore it to positive. The world needs this kind of conviction amongst its populace.

My clairvoyant abilities have often been put to the test by clients who were the victims of crimes, which helped build my experience with clairvoyant vision. One client, Ginger, had a black pearl heirloom necklace stolen. She told me only two things: she had two friends over one night and the next day she discovered that her valuable necklace was missing. First, I informed of both of her friends' physicality and personalities. One I identified as having red hair, the other of mixed race—a drinker and more adventurous.

Next I described the mindset of the criminal in the act—how she believed my client would assume the culprit was her other friend. But the innocent friend, who was

> I called Rebecca franticly because I misplaced $3,500. I didn't know what to do. I was lost! I didn't know if there was anything I could do. She said "hang on a minute."
>
> She was quiet a minute, then she said "I see shoes. It's somewhere in a shoe." Then she described a bag.
>
> I thought I had hidden it in a vase, but I went ahead and looked through all my shoeboxes for it and I still couldn't find it. I was devastated.
>
> A couple weeks later I was sitting on the end of my bed when I happened to look up. Hanging over my door was a plastic shoe caddy. My bag of money was in a zip loc bag between two shoes! It was right where she said it was; I just overlooked it.
>
> —Faith Wright

half-East Indian, believed in Karma and would never commit such a crime.

I described the redheaded friend's bedroom closet: shoe boxes—and inside those shoe boxes—hair nets. Inside one of those boxes was the missing necklace, which from time to time her teenage daughter snuck out to ogle.

All of my descriptions were right on target. My client confirmed to me that her friend keeps her hair nets in shoe boxes in the closet. It all fit. She corroborated that the culprit had longstanding emotional and financial difficulties. My client later thanked me for the information. "When a crucial piece of information is missing," she said, "you fill in the blank."

People don't always take my advice. A referral with raving reviews sent a woman, Carmine, to me for a half-hour phone consultation. I began by telling Carmine implicitly about herself and her husband, thereby bolstering my abilities as legitimate. She said she had one question.

I immediately reported that I'm getting a "no" impression. I explained how I have to go with my initial gut sense—my past accuracy dictates that—and that I stand by what I feel. Next, she asked if she should buy a building for a business venture.

Again, I emphatically pleaded with her: *no.* I explained why and the underlying fault lines of the situation. I talked about the building being unfit. She described the current owners who were selling the building as shady. She shared that in the past, she had been rash, gone against her gut and lost money.

Now she was about to fork over her life savings. I hoped I had stopped her from doing that. How often can you replace that? And timing is everything.

Despite what I said, I later heard from her friend that she went right ahead and bought it that very day. As I had forewarned, the building turned out to have severe issues—including black mold. It had to be leveled and I never heard from her again.

I'm not sure how many times I've been discounted over one's pirating pride, but mostly what I hear reported back to me is exactly how accurate my predictions have been. I have accurately predicted when peoples' babies would be born, when they would marry— along with accompanying descriptions of these people and events, even first names of those they'll be involved with — future jobs, homes...and countless details of their lives.

I have located missing pets, predicting when they will be back. I have also located missing wallets and money. Sometimes I am given the reward that was promised me; other times a surprise bonus after offering to do help for free—but best of all is a testimonial. I like this kind of work and believe it's what I was made for.

Sherri, a woman from a neighboring shop, dropped in to tell me her apartment had been broken into. I immediately began describing the perpetrator. I told her he has one foot larger than the other. I described his past modus operandi and many of his unique physical characteristics, including his illnesses, which is de rigueur for me. She could confirm everything I said because she knew him, including the fact that when the police measured the footprints he left behind on her carpet, one was markedly larger. This wasn't the first time he had burglarized her home.

Another shopkeeper-friend around the block has a vintage store. His store cat, Harriet, glams around on top of his glass cases in a pearl choker, greeting customers. His shop was broken into and all of his jewelry stolen.

One day, while I was lovingly squeezing the plump Harriet, I psychically flashed on a description of the *"angry man"* who had broken into and robbed the store. I relayed what I mentally perceived back to Eugene, who sadly confirmed that it matched the description of a man who had previously been in to sell him some gold and, low and behold, was caught later with some of his remaining, missing jewelry.

It is interesting for a psychic when animals are witnesses to a crime. Perception truly seems to have no boundaries. And as I have learned, it takes any route it can get to give us information we need at a critical moment. I imagine a lot of "dream" jobs that capitalize on my abilities. Just one example would be to help the Coast guard planes locate vessels or people lost at sea. I once expressed to a client how I feel like a caged bird.

When I sit outside in the summer to take a break, every now and then I notice and pick up how badly people need readings. I sense hidden health problems, souls trying to contact them and important events just around the corner. It hits my heart. But these people aren't after a psychic reading. They're in town to shop and eat.

This is an extremely strenuous profession. This work is systemic. Being a psychic is not "fun." In the simplest terms, it means I am extra susceptible to pain. For me it is the equivalent of being naked out in the world every day. I am like a humongous magnet and people are essentially prickly nails. Most impressions I pick up from people around me are not happy things. When I sense others' pain it can hurt me, but this also points me in a direction that enables me to do a lot of good things for people as well.

Sometimes in my office, I could hear people outside, loudly deprecating my work.

When I needed to step out for a break, I considerately put up a sign indicating how to reach me. That didn't keep people from walking up, seeing my sign and loudly making a joke at my expense: "Well, you think she would have *known* we were coming..."

My silent reply: "Exactly!"

People believe I am game for their abuse. I have been called every name in the book by those passing by (who never met me). A lot of their hatred is based in fear—in facing something they don't understand or in being exploited by someone pretending to be psychic.

I was truly blessed to have my mother beside me in her gallery as I learned to deal with all these situations, to brush off the detractors and to revel triumphantly in the expanding success stories.

Just as I was closing my window at the end of a long day a young woman presented and yelled up, "What do you charge?"

Screaming back was not my forte as a professional, but I knew she wasn't going to be a customer so I hollered back down my rate.

She said she was on a camping trip and "I always heard that if you have a gift you need to give it for free!" I knew she was trying to weasel her way out of paying and also that there was nothing critical going on to make me see her.

These kinds of people are not meant for me. I need people who will reward me in kind. I have real sharpness with the clarity of this information. I am a caregiver. I do feel terribly responsible for people, but I can't take all these people on. I have to be able to take care of myself.

What I do means way more to me than money. A wise client expressed that if I have a gift I have to *use* it. I don't have to give it away. I am looking at things that are uncomfortable to me.

Still, I thought about what she said. So at this time when I was learning more of the value of my medical intuition I paid for an ad in the paper and ran it twice that I would give free readings to the poor. I did not want to restrict my practice to the wealthier. I knew that the people who were poor needed the help the most. I didn't get a single response.

A tourist popped in who wanted to get a look at me but was undecided. I gave her my brief introduction covering my services. "I may return tomorrow—I'm not sure my husband will let me." That is always a signal that it's a no—when they plop the word "husband" in the middle of it. She seemed very sad as she walked away. She was nice. I felt for her and at the same time was alerted to an issue. Some people don't realize when they need to take advantage of an opportunity before them.

I got up and looked down the way for her. "Excuse me—can you come back here for a moment?" I knew something was wrong. She smiled as she turned back. I told her I just needed to talk to her—not charge her—to tell her I sensed she needed to be careful about a particular area of her breast.

In response she told me she had breast cancer in the past and they put markers in her breasts four years ago in certain areas to continually screen, but she will not go back! I talked to her, listened, and encouraged her to follow through for herself. At the end of the day I'm still a messenger. For the record, if I hadn't gone to work as a psychic, I would still be delivering messages to people—or the masses.

For me, this is a burning passion. Some days, I just *have to* tell someone what I sense will happen. Sometimes, I just *have to* give a reading, just to give this burbling energy an outlet. It's more than just abilities. It's an actual calling.

Several years after starting my business my reputation grew and I no longer relied strictly on tourists, which was a relief. One afternoon a man who appeared to have just jumped from the back of a truck after hitchhiking a ride from a Grateful Dead concert wearing sixties-era patchwork overalls and two long, bleached Rasta braids planted himself directly below my window. Pointing his index fingers on adjacent sides of his temple he loudly rang out "Am I going to see you?" Of course, some people don't take me seriously. Next time I turned around he was gone.

And that is one of the more interesting aspects about my being there. There are people who need me—the peace that I have offer. There is healing in store for them.

The greatest part of what I do is the people who I get to help. They say they feel drawn into my place, often saying they got a good feeling from my sign.

Most have received a type of spiritual cleansing that they deeply needed and couldn't receive by any other means. I am very grateful for their belief in me. We all share a common goal of making the world a better place. I hope you understand that *this* is what being a psychic is really about.

🏵 15 Fifteen Minutes of Fame

Mental communication without verbaliza-
tion ... all space is made up of waves and
we are constantly sending and receiving
messages from our brain.

—*Tina Louise*

I extended an offer of a free reading to a local radio host because I liked her good-naturedness and verve on the air. She showed up at my office in a cute hat and the reading was a success. She called me up to invite me to be interviewed live on her program; my first media appearance.

She said, "I am a skeptic, but I felt there was something *different* about you—the things you said were so accurate. I was so blown away I had to go home and think about it all for a while. I can tell that what you do comes from the light and not the dark."

It would be the first time the station had hosted a psychic. In promotions of my upcoming appearance, she told listeners, "She knew things that no one could have known—and I mean *no one.* She is sincere. She is an authentic psychic!"

This was my first "break" and I prayed that I would do well. The day of the show I was nervous and afraid I would feel flummoxed about how to answer the callers' questions. I was happy to discover I could perform psychically over the airwaves.

A woman asked me if she was pregnant. I answered, "No—not this time around." She then told me her husband had a vasectomy. Well, what do you know? They did not air this call; too much information.

I found it easy to read people over the airwaves from the radio station. Environment can have an immediate effect on my ability to discern psychically. Being in the radio station magnified the intensity, clarity and speed of my perceptions. We were underground, cushioned from noise and other distracting elements, which helped make my intuition crystal clear.

A smattering of callers wanted to know when they would "hook up" romantically. I guess to them it was very serious.

Then a college student called in, asking three questions mashed

> *I've had the opportunity to meet with Rebecca Bartlett quite a few times in the past few years and have really come to appreciate and respect her God-given talent as a psychic. She comes from a very good place and has a wonderful heart.*
>
> *My first reading with her blew me away with some details she brought up that she couldn't have known ahead of time. My father had passed and I wanted a connection. She got "in tune" with him and told me he was thankful for a letter I had written to him after he passed away! No one knew of that note but me! She also told me about two babies my parents had lost...and indeed, my mom had had two miscarriages before I was born.*
>
> *I've had Rebecca on the air with me during the Retro Lunch Hour on B97 more than once and have been blown away at the connection she makes with listeners just through phone conversations!*
>
> —Pam Thrash

into one. *Should she go to Mexico or not? If not, should she veg out on her roommate's sofa for a year? Or should she go back to school?*

I reached into my empathic body for what I needed to tell her. "Don't go to Mexico," I said. I was surprised at the information I received next, but I learned long ago never to second-guess myself to judge whether or not the message made sense. So I added: "You will travel internationally and then work for the C.I.A."

To our astonishment, she excitedly announced: "They already tried recruiting me!" Adding, "I studied Arabic in college." Within a month of my radio appearance, the news featured a hellacious border war in Mexico; hundreds were shot or kidnapped. A month after that, swine flu outbreaks resulted in quarantines and deaths.

I was so relieved that I got things right on my first live engagement and even made a profound prediction or two.

The hour-long interview flew by. "Wow!" Pam exclaimed on air, "Would you like to come back?" The next time I was appeared on the program, the theme of the show was "predictions." Pam made it clear we would stick to personal and not world events. It was the afternoon of New Year's Eve and the callers presented inane questions, such as whether or not their parties would be busted by the police that night. I don't think any of the questions were even serious enough to be aired. It was a lackluster show, but it was fun working with Pam and afterward several listeners called asking for a reading—which made it worthwhile.

Before the show, Pam asked me off-air if she would be safe on her upcoming flight. I hesitated. I told her I wasn't worried about her flight but that I sensed that May would be a dangerous time to fly. It was indeed. That May retaliations were underway due to the capturing of the world's most-wanted man.

❀ 16 Medical Intuition

There is an empathic element in the physical body of the intuitive, as well as a visual diagnostic aspect.

—Russell Targ

I have been a floater throughout my life, experimenting with different hats in the medical field. At one point in my life I felt I had to see the inside of the human body and engage in the work of repairing it. I studied surgical technology and radiologic technology and saw everything and then some, only to recoil at the sterile environment and pain around me. I could not separate from it. That was not meant to be my place, but everything I learned, from pharmacology, anatomy, biology, microbiology, and ethics was invaluable in my understanding of how the medical system should perform and how the body heals or gets sick.

At that time I would never have imagined I would end up as a professional psychic, but I believe education is never wasted. It's one of the most important things you can give yourself and others. My hope is that we will make the world a better place with our knowledge and restore it to balance.

Things have come full circle for me. As a psychic training on the job, my threshold expanded along the way—peaking as my body and mind developed into new striations of sensitivities. When my latest "discovery" unfolded it was as though a completely new way of looking at things developed in my sensory repertoire—in a single moment.

One second I was reading a client and the very next my hands were plying the air—reaching amidst the aura like a wand at a security check point. My hands began to undulate over all the different areas of this person's auric field—or bio-field—deciphering minute disturbances as they gravitated toward a compromised area.

This "catch" indicates something is out of order and needs mending. My mind can then name it. I decided to call this process a *body scan*. Low-and-behold, I wasn't the first to coin that term.

Clients seem to enjoy a pleasant sensation as I move my hands around their auras. I mostly start at the top and move my hands all the way down, citing physical illnesses, emotional thought patterns, including crucial events they've experienced in their lives—making pronouncements as I go:

"You had asthma as a child but it's cleared up now."

"Your left ovary has been cauterized."

"You've had a miscarriage."

"You had a lumpectomy in this breast."

"This knee has been operated on."

"You are diabetic."

"You are sensitive to microwaves." (Client had a pacemaker.)

I sense what's hidden from view with extraordinary precision. I would say I consider what I'm doing to be similar to some kind of ultrasound. People feel warm sensations when I perform this energy scan. One client called it my "sonar."

At times I click my fingers to create more pulsations of energy reverberating for my ESP to digest—intensifying the scan—much as a dolphin uses its own sonar. There should be no slacking;

it's best when I really breathe and incorporate much of my own energy into the process.

This reminded me of radiesthesia, or dowsing, which has been practiced for thousands of years on every continent, typically in rural environments. (The controls behind the ability have been attributed to everything from electromagnetism and radiation to subconscious readings of the site, but at the end of the day, its origins are unknown.)

> *"I have been around intuitives for nearly 30 years, and I have never seen anyone do what Rebecca does. Just by moving her hands through the air around my body, she picked up on specific physical conditions and even family issues from far, far back."*
>
> —Joy

Ninety-seven percent of my business comes from word-of-mouth advertising, with clients referring their friends and family after they've been to see me. Brigette was one of those rare clients who came in after seeing the small sign on the exterior of my building. She contacted me later and shared her feedback with a testimonial:

"Rebecca informed me of three specific health issues I wasn't even aware I had. I did seek the care of my doctor and resolved these issues…When I met Rebecca I was filled with a sense of peace…I feel blessed to have found Rebecca!"

I contacted her to request more information. People very seldom provide specific details in their testimonials—most share about how I made them feel. So, she paraphrased for me. "I saw you in July of 2009. You described an issue with my left breast, and a month later I found a small lump/nodule in my left breast. I went to my NP who then ordered a mammogram and the results identified a cyst… "

When I saw Brigette again, I asked her to clarify the *specific* location of the cyst. She pointed where my hand had "hovered—"

as she put it—directly over an area that's just to the side and above the afflicted breast, near the armpit.

"Your hand waved over right here," she said, eyes wide. It turns out this is a part of the underarm area a lot of women don't check themselves.

Another way this modality can help is for a person who may need to recall experiences lost to amnesia or unconsciousness.

The aura for me is an interesting kind of medical "horoscope." Clients have told me I expressed something that happens after the timeframe of their visit. In these incidences, future circumstances vibrate off a "warning" to me. Clients would stop me in town and say, "You were right, you were right. You told me the name of a test and it turned out that was exactly what I needed..." Again, this comes without any input from clients. Energy projects—period. I have an inkling that what we refer to as "psychic" is just how our senses interact or interplay within dimensions around us—perhaps of time—of which we still have little understanding. Hence, the déjà vu experience. Interestingly, I have never seen colors around a person's aura—ever. In the case of watching a television program with contestants of any sort I can ordinarily pick up who is going to win based on what I "see" from their auras. I envision a light, halo-effect surrounding the body—or a lack thereof.

For someone who is about to take home a prize, I pick up on this near future event by visually scanning for a vaporous shimmering flow in the current of energy around a client's aura. For someone who is about to have his hopes dashed, my underlying senses perceive a grey smudginess instead. This demarcates basic dread around him. Think about it—an emotional reaction so strong that one's energy is already being affected by it. And I scoop it up. It's just a matter of mine being the prickliest of senses and perceptions. It's also interesting when you realize that in the physical world there are no colors, just waves of different lengths. We don't really see color, we see light. Light is a form of energy and it travels in waves. All existing things have vibrations. We release and magnify energy. It's easily transmitted to other existing things.

Vibration is life.

Working one Easter, my finger stopped and hovered over one particular area of a woman's colon. I pointed at a spot to indicate my concern. "There is something wrong with the energy here," I said.

This client later wrote: "While doing a body scan, you targeted a specific area that should be watched. Six months later, with very minor symptoms, I was diagnosed with colon cancer. Because of you, I had scheduled a colonoscopy instead of ignoring it. Thankfully, I had surgery and since it hadn't spread to my pancreas, lymphatic system, or liver, no oncology [chemotherapy treatment] was necessary. Thank you for my life, Rebecca!"

I won't allow a single client to give me any information up front about medical problems they are experiencing. I want to sense it independently—on my own terms—to elicit greater accuracy. A medical worker asks a patient for symptoms whereas I intuit them to get inside for a first-hand look around. It's not guess work—it's sense work. The gradient of my perceptions abstains from any logical thought process. It's much deeper. In fact I loosen the ropes on my consciousness just enough that I may not recall everything I just said. The client is required to let go and let loose, too. I get *in the zone* and we connect our conscious energies.

I was performing a body scan on a teacher wearing thick blue jeans. I pointed to a spot on her right thigh and said with an imploring voice, "Of course you'll need to verify this with a doctor —but I feel you have got something vascular wrong 'here' in your leg."

She responded, "Yes I do, and I had to have a stent put in—right where you're pointing."

A client sent her older sister in for a reading. I gave her a body scan, starting at the top, as usual, with her head. Because the original client was an influential person, I was nervous about whether I would get everything right. As soon as I began scanning her energy field I mentally picked up the words "brain cancer" and I thought, *Oh, no. Oh, no.* How do I handle this? I can't just say "cancer" to someone! Besides the fact that I am not a physician and I can't diagnose anyone one way or the other, I was always cautious about bringing up negative outcomes.

I pursed my lips and continued—mortified by dread. This is not something I ever want to be wrong about and another hitch is that I can't *always* know with certainty if the disease is currently active or energetic leftovers from the past. I didn't say anything at first, carefully holding back until I figured out the most ethical way to approach it.

I was waiting for the right words to say, but the second I stalled near the completion of her aura reading she asked me, "Is my brain cancer going to come back?" She was so worried. How could I answer that kind of question? I won't say things that are frightening and I don't just want to predict illness; I want to help prevent it. I was just at a loss of what to say.

I read about dogs being able to detect cancer cells. In 2004, British physicians discovered that dogs can identify bladder cancer patients by smells in urine. And in 2006, California doctors reported that dogs can identify breast and lung cancers by smell. But I never imagined it would happen to me, too—albeit with a different "sense" than smell.

A physical body scan is by no means the only way I "see" into a medical situation, it's just another way I learned—a form of psychic *adaptation.*

A client can simply ask me for more information about the state of his or her health, or the health of someone they know, and I will focus my intuition, using clairvoyance, on a particular area or the entire body, regardless of whether they're present or not.

With one of my repeat clients, a retired politician, I "scanned up" her son, with my ability to read him by proxy. I said, "There is something *off* with his left testicle."

She confirmed, "Yes, there is something *off* there! *He had it removed,* and, yes, I do think it was his left side." She left my office, not for the first time, with tears in her eyes "Rebecca, you are amazing—your gifts are phenomenal." Another bear hug from an appreciative client.

Tracy was one of the many core people with a blend of German and Native American ancestry in this Indiana population. High cheek bones,

> *I have spent four years with American medical professionals that could not determine the cause of, control, or cure my medical issues. As such, I began looking for a legitimate medical intuitive for help and found Rebecca. She identified the root cause, the right doctor(s), and proper diet for me. She did not speak in generalities. This information was highly specific. She even spoke of a currently existing medical device, yet to be approved, that will revolutionize treatment of my condition.*
>
> *I followed her direction and everything happened just as she said it would. And now for the first time in years my condition is stable, under control and improving. In fact, during my first visit with a "new" doctor, I was informed of a new medical device, just as she described, that is presently on the cusp of approval...When you contact Rebecca you will receive useable, concise, in depth, accurate information that goes well beyond anything you expected. Worth every penny and more.*
>
> *I hope she continues with this work. A heck of a lot of people out there will really benefit from it.*
>
> —C.S. Geologist

acorn-hued skin, vivid blue eyes and a razor-sharp wit. She came in to ask about her friend who was in trouble. Knowing only that her friend was in an abusive relationship, and *absolutely nothing* about her physical condition or health, I nonetheless warned her outright of several medical issues, including a right-side kidney infection. Later that day, the friend called me, worried. Tracy drove her to the hospital.

I received a phone call a couple hours later from the friend. "I've just been to the ER and they told me I have a right-side kidney infection."

Some people might find it strange that people would come to a psychic for a "health reading," but my clients who have gotten results from me don't question whether it's strange. They often make the same comment to me: "Why not use every tool?" This is the resolve of my clients—taking an affirmative stance—wanting to be as strong as possible.

Acute connections happen as much over the phone. I don't ever pump a caller for information. At times I name the diagnoses they have already been given, but more usually I relate the symptoms a caller is experiencing.

As begins every phone reading, I asked a client to speak her name aloud. Then I took a moment to receive my impressions. After feeling inside myself—via empathy—for what was going on in her body I cited her illnesses: a herniated disc, fibromyalgia and diabetes. When she asked about her foster child, I told her I felt that he is affected by autism and described his other ailments as well, which she confirmed. Most everyone I work with remarks at how much they think this takes out of me. Yes, they are right, which is why I keep a light schedule and need at least an hour break in-between my sessions.

A man with a thick foreign accent called, sounding unsure and emotionally reserved. It was winter, slow season for me. I needed his business so I had to push my abilities into overdrive.

Take it from me, he wasn't giving me much energy output, so it was up to me to invest my faith in the process. Remember, it takes two to make a psychic reading.

I pulled in his sluggish energy and began rattling off a little list of conditions. Now, on this one occasion I might have had an aid. As I sat there trying so hard to feel his comatose energy response (it's always iffy perceptively when there's a skeptic involved) I glanced at myself in the large mirror that was sitting on the floor—an ornate Victorian piece I found at a barn sale to restore. It was too heavy to hang.

Looking at my image, I reflexively noted—internally— through mental focus, places that mirrored the corresponding trouble spots on his body. Voila! I sensed something on his tongue and described the precise area. He replied that he had a doctor's appointment the very next day about the exact spot. It was his chief concern. I never used the mirror again, though. That could be considered an apparatus of some sort.

I kept building my range psychically. Had I never gone into business and had these experiences, I probably never would have discovered how much I was capable of doing. I imagine all of it was building up and waiting for its release.

In my entire time working as a psychic, there have been a handful of people I couldn't connect with at all. I don't want to be kind of good or to just pass muster. It is rare that someone exhibits a negative attitude about my readings. I always have to talk them out of paying me and normally, they are so grateful about my honesty and ending the session that they send their friends to see me.

In a scenario where I am blocked I usually stop immediately, but in one case a man came to see me who had been referred by a very loyal client of mine and I did not just want to send him packing. When he called from Indianapolis to schedule an appointment, he sounded extremely jittery. He told me he couldn't really make sense of any of this, he wasn't sure he believed in psychics. However, I had come so highly recommended he thought he'd give it a whirl. When he showed up he remarked being nervous to a degree I won't repeat. I knew then I was going to have an impossible time of it.

I would make the effort, at least.

I could not help but notice that when he walked in his legs were grotesquely swollen. He suffered from diabetes and was struggling with alcohol dependency. I have noticed that when someone is actively using any mind-altering substance it can block my clear reception. He didn't want to go to the doctor because he was afraid of what he might be told. I told him I thought he should see a doctor, but that was it. I wanted to help if I could, but this man's nerves cut off most of the insight I could offer him. Human emotional energy is strong and his fear cut me right out. Almost like a case of psychic constipation.

At the end of the session I told him I felt his reading was nowhere close to as accurate as I would have liked, something he could not have known by means of comparison, and I refused to take his payment.

Oddly enough, the following day, alarm bells went off in my head. The man from yesterday; his name and his face flashed across my mental screen: *venal thrombosis—going to affect the lung*. What was I going to do? I really want to make a difference in my clients' lives and want them to have faith in my abilities, but I couldn't read him when he was in my presence. Now I was getting input that could actually help save him, if my impressions were correct. When I care in the beginning, I continue to care even when they're gone. This X-factor to me comes straight from the heart.

I soon heard from the mutual friend who shared that he had made it to a doctor in the nick of time to be treated for the exact same medical issue I had received in my flash of insight. That's just how ESP works. Not always when you want it and not always when you expect it. I just respect the process, have no fear, and leave it alone.

I have pointed out so many breast cysts, former locations of cysts and tumors that I have lost count. I have sensed them on people and on pets. I have, not surprisingly, tried at every twist and turn to have a doctor or someone open within the scientific community document my abilities, going back to the first time I discovered my abilities with psychometry.

Determined and naive, I responded to an ad in the college student newspaper purportedly looking for subjects who have "ESP." I was so excited to find that. When I called I told the man who answered, "I'm psychic and I would like to be in your study."

His response left a sour impression. "We don't believe in psychics," he said, "this is a study on *schizotypal personality disorder.*" I wonder how many subjects had they gotten to come in?

When based solely on opinion, which is superficial, clinicians may falsely pathologize intuition. Current diagnostic categories cannot classify this fairly. (There are still no genetic tests, brain scans, bio markers or lab tests.) It's just too subjective.

An important factor to consider in accepting someone's psychic sureness or authenticity is that there is a learning curve he will go through in differentiating true impressions from subconscious recollections, fears and distractions. And everyone has those. The same holds true of precognitive dreams; being able to determine if a dream is foretelling an actual future event or if it's a "dud" conjured up by the same factors as above. I'm not suggesting it doesn't have its limitations, but nonetheless it is real. It doesn't distort our regular senses, it enhances them.

And normal people who are psychic don't think they have great powers over other people. And there will always be individuals who say they are "psychic" who are not, but that is another problem entirely. (For further information refer to appendix II, How to Recognize a True Psychic.)

People have suggested that oncologists would be interested in my work. But imagine what I'm up against. I can't just cold-call doctors.

My mother thought she found someone willing to help me. She met him at an art reception. A local professor, he was a nuclear physicist and neuroscientist originally from California who came to our university. He met with me in my office to discuss consciousness and my abilities.

"We physicists are all skeptics," he confessed. He explained how he never used to believe in any of these phenomena until one day deep meditation changed his view and later he began focusing on consciousness studies.

At the end of our conversation, he wanted to test me. I had been hoping and expecting he would, since that was the whole point: confirmation. Nervously, I went to task, performing a body scan. As I gave him my results, he declared assuredly, "You passed my test." I nailed it. That was a relief, because he had one of the sternest, most serious, critical countenances I had ever encountered, but he was very nice. It was just the scientist in him. In these situations (testing) I usually have to put my abilities in overdrive, because it's not a natural exchange.

I pushed my cause, but he said he couldn't think of anyone at the university who would be willing to set up a study. The psychology department, especially, would have "deaf ears" to me, he cautioned. He strongly urged me to begin compiling a list of all my predictions, which spurred me to begin asking for testimonials.

Then, at the end of our visit, he added protectively, "Keep doing what you're doing." That is what science is all about; making inroads to try to connect the dots and *explain* the unknown.

17 A Heart for Healing

*Your body is not who you are. The mind and
spirit transcend the body.*

—*Christopher Reeve*

When I'm working with psychic energy, one thing leads to another.
It builds. It was obvious to me that if I could get in touch with
people's energy—feel it, explicitly connect with it—that I might
be able to *manipulate* it through this interactive contact. Could
I extend the ability I have to sense peoples' illnesses into helping
them to heal?

I put my theory to the test, practicing on a nasty festering
wound I received from pulling out weeds bare-handed. From
necessity came invention. I put myself in a state where I felt
anything was possible. I stilled myself and let my heart lead
me. I just allowed nature to take its course—to direct me how
to manifest a healing. I was determined not to be a prisoner
of my pain and shackled in my body when I have this special
sense of touch and mind-energy waiting to do something more
productive.

I coursed my energy toward my injury. I focused very hard
on the effected site, singing to it, if you will, changing the state
of its energy. Using all the energy in my cells, my mind and the

pure strength and willpower driven by the emotions of my heart, I attempted to heal my wound.

Before my very eyes, the wound diminished. The pus, the blood and the scab all reduced to a tiny pink mark.

I made it vanish with my mind and with my breath. It was the most amazing thing I had seen in my life! *This was the hallmark of feeling and utilizing psychic energy.* This is energy's greatest good.

> *Rebecca, I am amazed that you were able to detect my health problems by phone. I am astounded that you were able to send energy to me by telepathy. I could feel the heat and energy radiate in my body. You are the real thing.*
>
> — Sylvia

I proved that thoughts are a force. When you really understand that we control our body and that our thoughts can work for us, it is not inconceivable. We must not underestimate the power of our thoughts and our energy. After all, what is love if not energy you feel and send out? Does the "intangible" energy produced by love not create a powerful affect?

The mind can be extravagant in pushing the limits of its uses. It brings to mind those real-life stories of youngsters lifting cars off a parent trapped underneath.

I began using this concentrated healing energy to benefit people. The warm, tingling sensations flowing from my hands as I concentrate localized energy is comes from the same place as the energy used in aura readings—it's just a different tact. Sometimes I think of particular colors of light and focus it in an area.

Once when I began working to end a woman's acute respiratory pain I felt something take place in my body. Suddenly I felt I was literally both floating and ten feet tall. It was such an overpowering relief and release! At last, I didn't have to channel only my own energy to help someone, which was exhausting work,

I had help. I have no idea how or from whom the power came from. I don't have an explanation for everything that happens. It is still a mystery to me.

During our session I noticed my client's face relax into a calmed expression. Immediately afterwards she shared with me how she felt a cool, refreshing mist of air envelop her and that she saw flashes of yellow, purple and green lights around me. Her pain and inability to breathe from asthma ceased. I assumed this was temporary. I learned and practiced this skill, but I felt uncomfortable making any claims that I could heal. This was not the focus of my work.

From time to time I continued using the healing energy on my own. I cleared up an eye infection while I was away from home and unable to see a doctor with a loud humming that sounded like something very primal—it came up from within me, not unlike a scream. I instinctively knew what kind of energy to put on it to flush it out. When there's a will, there's a way.

I worked on my dog the night I adopted her home from the shelter. She was extremely stressed and had an abscess from a surgical wound that wasn't healing. She reacted like she was mildly hypnotized and experiencing something tonic and euphoric. She basically went under as though she had been given ether. Her body soaked it up.

When my cat had ear mites I gave it a try on her. She didn't take to it at all like my dog. Instead of sinking into a stupor, she became alert and sniffed the air just around my fingertips as if she were picking up an obscure foreign scent. I wonder what caused her to sniff the air so curiously. Well, there was no way Puff kitty was going to let me dabble on her.

There have been many things I've learned to do—directed perhaps by some higher guidance, instinct, or curiosity. But being able to heal has been the most surprising. Yet Yogis have been harnessing this energy for centuries. Like them, I use breathing work when I'm changing or trying to course energy. This is all just part of nature—our nature and our body's intrinsic ability to correct and restore itself.

I have unlocked a gift we have all been given. We all fight all the time to stay alive and our awareness is key to that fight. Be aware and learn, and you can do anything you put your mind to. Life is really a journey of discovery. Release your inhibitions and be accepting. You'll be surprised what you can learn.

Psychic ability is the sense that tells the truth, cutting through all of the illusions of sight, sound and touch.

Psychic ability immerses those of us lucky and hardworking enough to use it into a new dimension of sight, sound and touch—a quantum wonderland of discovery.

Psychic ability is not hard and it's not that mystifying. It isn't really off-limits to anyone. There are dimensions beyond ours and everything that goes along with that adds an inescapable context to our lives—if we let it.

18 A Blessing in Disguise

Never bend your head. Always hold it high.
Look the world straight in the eye.

—Helen Keller

I left my alcove in Nashville and rented a tiny suite in Bloomington. Again, no neon street sign, but doing what I love in a professional manner, even donning a dress suit.

It's interesting how what seems at first like small annoyances can have a greater significance. Eventually you find out why. Word to the wise: Don't look at the messenger, just the message. One day I was in a tiny but popular health-foods deli. It was the lunch hour and every table was occupied. On my tray was a bowl of hot soup. I was frustrated when I realized that one of the tables was occupied by a Pentecostal prayer group, drinking complimentary glasses of water. Freeloaders—why weren't they eating like paying customers?

A red-headed stranger in line checking out ahead of me generously offered to let me sit with her. During lunch I opened up and shared with her what I did for a living. It turned out she was a massage therapist who was very marketing-savvy. Straightaway she told one person who worked in her building about me—who also happened to be a gainfully-employed massage therapist. From that tip I received the only business I had for months at a time and connections that have lasted years.

As a new business person to the area and without a budget for advertising, my prospects were slim. Without this one happenstance I would not have eaten *anywhere* for much longer. Well what do you know: *The Lord works in mysterious ways.*

One afternoon I got a phone call asking if I would be interested in being interviewed. I finally got press—a front-page feature in a large university newspaper. I encouraged the reporter, Danielle Paquette, to bring a subject for me to demonstrate my abilities. In this venue seeing is believing, and I was keen not to have people discount what I do.

Danielle brought in a handful of photographs and accompanying questions. I explained the personalities and medical conditions of these people for her.

"Wow! You can do that with just a photograph?" When she asked me where she would work in the future, I named the cities of Atlanta and New York to her short list. I also implored her, "You *have* to keep writing. "

Danielle spent about two hours thoroughly interviewing me that cold, rainy night until the time came to usher in the subject so I could demonstrate an aura reading.

Regarding the subject to be read, I insisted I did not want any information ahead of time and I implored her to send me someone who was neither nervous nor skeptical.

I was alarmed by how absolutely petrified this girl named Nicole was. "I'm not nervous," she masqueraded. Later I would read in the article that she had been sent in to see me on a dare.

I had to read on pure faith alone because her auric body was "stunned speechless." For me it was akin to driving blind. Normally I can feel teeny pulse-like sensations that burble in the tips of my fingers as I direct my hands through the crosshairs of a person's out-flowing of empathy. Her aura felt barren of the open energy I need to tap into. Still, I had to keep trying to do my best.

Normally, when something is wrong in someone's aura, I am guided by a force that I can feel, pulling me in, like a pendulum's turn. But when people are nervous, they pull their energy in, making it a tricky thing for me to force with someone so unwilling. It needs to be a two-way connection.

The first impression I picked up was her fear of drowning. I said, "You just hate being under water." I needed to know if I was even in the right ballpark, given how afraid she was and how off-limits her energy felt to me. If I was correct, then I could go further in trusting my intuition. Danielle sat in the back corner of my office, dutifully inscribing notes.

To my great relief her eyes widened in response as she nodded up and down, glancing over at the reporter in stunned disbelief. She let out a deep breath that finally allowed her tension to dissipate, in turn discharging more of her bio-energy for me to absorb through my psychic feelers.

As Danielle described it:

Bartlett closed her eyes and began twisting and turning her hands in the space around Nicole's body. "Your white blood cells are back to where they should be." Nicole pursed her lips and nodded. She had undergone chemotherapy less than a year earlier, which wreaked havoc on her immune system... Bartlett continued to trace lines in the air, as though reading an invisible trail of Braille. "Did you have something bad, and did it somehow affect your fallopian tubes?" Nicole paused. "Yes," she said. Doctors discovered a malignant tumor on her ovaries.

When she left, Nicole was flushed with excitement, giggling and wowed. Danielle next turned to tracking down and interviewing some of my clients who agreed to share more first-hand accounts for the record.

A few days later, the newspaper's staff photographer called and he and Danielle tried to take my picture, but the camera would not function. At this point Danielle also broke the news that out of two hours of recording on the paper's highest-tech equipment, only twenty minutes of my voice registered. We both observed the red "record" light on the whole time. This has happened to me before—whatever energy is interworking has been known to interfere with or stop the regularity of electronic devices.

When "The Psychic Next Door" hit the stands on February 3, 2010, my picture was framed in pitch black on the front page. The caption read: "Local aims to heal, help." The article was positive.

The reporter who wrote the story was recently named National Writing Champion, winning the Hearst Award, which is for students what the Pulitzer Prize is for career journalists. And, her big internship first came with CNN in Atlanta, followed by work in New York.

Among those who came to see me after the article hit the stands were veteran professors and students from all walks of life. I was informed by a medical student who came to me for a reading that she happened to read a letter to the editor following my story. So I dug through the recycling bin to find the previous week's paper and was shocked at what I read—that it was actually printed after I offered to be tested to further prove I was legit. A biology student named Chris M., *who had never met or previously heard of me*, marched in to the paper with his opinion piece. He pronounced me a "fraud" who did "cold readings." (I had to look up just precisely what cold readings meant.) He dismissed the testimony of my clients who were contacted by the reporter. He twisted what happened in the blind subject demonstration, re-arranging quotes to negate their value. Chris M. is studying to be a scientist so let us turn to science to answer him in the next chapter.

Many of those throughout history with higher callings to serve mankind have openly shared an appreciation for their intuition, whether awake or in dreams, as it can help guide and guard us. One of these was Abraham Lincoln. I awoke in the middle of the night to record an automatic writing inspired by him. I recite it below.

"Words can terrorize through their unstructured, malevolent, radicalized views on the laws of nature, physics and mankind. Throughout time has been a desire to understand and work with the better parts of our nature, the intuition that lies deep inside of us. Fear will not lead us to an answer. Intimidation will make us turn astray from the truth that currently lies beyond our grasp. Hate will not point us in the direction needed to further a rational study of these scientific pursuits or to formulate a meaningful dialogue that stays true to science, not conflicted by those who speak out of context of knowledge of the experience of psi. It cannot be determined without foreknowledge what potential abilities belong to another individual. To speak of someone without a grasp of the facts and with an exclusion of the pertinent details can only lead to slander. Stay true to your words, they will serve you well, better than to sling hateful insults at individuals whose purpose here on earth is to serve to benefit society by reaching higher with their minds, not cowering in a corner for fear of reproach by their peers. There is one way to prove psychic ability for those who possess it with more attunement: Listen to them and their stories. Such a story was written about Rebecca Bartlett. Those who refuse to absorb the details temporarily lost their marbles. We, as a nation, owe a great debt to those who forge a path of honor through the attributes of any individual strength that allows them to conquer evil, though they themselves may be punished in the process of these higher goals. It cannot be left for history alone to analyze our strengths and weaknesses as a society that must muster our reserves of courage at every turn to overcome defeat; sometimes the breath of angels may be heard from amidst the clouds of those undeserving to carry the weight of such a gift. Let humanity be the judge of what is right or wrong. In the end, those who have the courage to make a difference are the ones who stand alone through time, forming a necessary bridge between present, past and future."

❀ 19 Psi in Science

"There are sadistic scientists who hurry to hunt down errors instead of establishing the truth."

—Marie Curie

This chapter reviews some of the science published by credible researchers into the psychic phenomenon known in science as *psi*.

Psi exists in different manifestations, including precognition, clairvoyance, telepathy, and psychokinesis. There have been, and continue to be, many scientific studies conducted in the area of psi, and the evidence is mounting.

In *The Conscious Universe: The Scientific Truth of Psychic Phenomena*, Dean Radin, Ph.D., tells us that "psi has been shown to exist in thousands of experiments. There are disagreements over how to interpret the evidence, but the fact is that virtually all scientists who have studied the evidence, *including the hard-nosed skeptics*, now agree that something interesting is going on that merits serious attention."

Top-rated scientific magazines have published peer-reviewed studies confirming psi, and five different U.S. government-sponsored scientific review committees have reviewed and examined the evidence for psi effects. All five concluded the evidence merits scientific study.

In 1995, Jessica Utts, a statistician at the University of California, Davis, reviewed formerly classified CIA psi research. Again, from Radin's book, we hear her conclusions:

> *The Statistical results of the studies examined are far beyond what is expected by chance. Arguments that these results could be due to methodological flaws in the experiments are soundly refuted. Effects of similar magnitude to those found in government- sponsored research …have been replicated at a number of laboratories across the world. Such consistency cannot be readily explained by claims of flaws or fraud.…It is recommended that future experiments focus on understanding how this phenomenon works, and on how to make it as useful as possible. There is little benefit to continuing experiments designed to offer proof.*

Some individual psi experiments have produced results with odds against chance greater than a billion to one. A *billion* to one.

Like many other functions of our brain and mind, such as dreaming and memory, we can't currently explain how ESP works.

Historically, academic researchers refrained from openly avowing psychic interest because it was associated with "nonmaterialistic" issues. To justify their research, scientists needed to discover a link to materialistic, known concepts. Investigations into finding a physical, scientific based explanation for paranormal mental phenomena occurred at the end of the nineteenth century led by the Soviets at Leningrad University and followed closely by the British Society for Psychical Research.

Even Nobel Prize recipient Ivan Pavlov became interested in these investigations as he referenced some unusual abilities observed in both man and animals. It wasn't long before the Soviets rallied a team of scientists, comprised of physiologists, physicists, psychologists, mathematicians, cyberneticians, neuro-biologists, and electronic engineers to investigate and find practical applications.

An elaborate compilation can be found in the previously classified report prepared by the *U.S. Air Force Systems Command Foreign Technology Division* for the *Defense Intelligence Agency* entitled "Paraphysics R&D—Warsaw Pact." It extensively uncovers the laboratory research and hypotheses advanced that our own scientists pried from behind the iron curtain during the cold war race of the '70's and '80's. (I downloaded it from a CD supplied with the book *The Seventh Sense: The Secrets of Remote Viewing as Told by a "Psychic Spy" for the U.S. Military*, by Lyn Buchanan.)

We have assumed that time is only linear. An early explanation involved a quantum physics concept—the "neutrino hypothesis." Because neutrinos have quantum characteristics of "spin"—the wide range of discharge frequencies could account for a basic interaction mechanism. This suggested all people could be interlinked by a neutrino field, calling to question established theories regarding time and space. In this idea of "closed time," past and future become relative beyond even the theory of relativity.

Paraphysics theorist G.A. Sergeyev considered the brain to be of a "paracrystal" nature able to emit and absorb electromagnetic radiation along with quasi-gravitational waves and affects.

Resistance by the establishment remained high as they searched to find a common denominator, or an information carrier and receptor mechanism. Quantum models continued to be considered along with other possibilities.

The discovery of electromagnetic waves occurred in 1888.

The brain is an electrical organ, having billions of neurons, or brain cells, each of which is extremely sensitive to electrical signals fired off by their neighbors. This accounts for our sensitivity to even tiny electromagnetic fields. During an EEG (electroencephalogram) test, electrodes detect the electrical signals transmitted between brain cells and record patterns of activity. This is a measure of the electrical processes that generate consciousness. Interestingly, the EEG machine was developed by Hans Berger in an attempt to learn how brains send signals and to unravel the nature of telepathy.

Some have conjectured that there may be electromagnetic waves of a certain unknown length emitted by the brain. This would be an unknown "metaetherial energy." One of the paradoxes they cited was that telepathic communication is independent of distance. Whatever this energy is, it does not seem to dissipate in space. They researched what could be responsible for telepathic signals, and if it could be amplified.

In the intervening years, the Czechs also worked to identify the source/s of biological energy. Dubrov, a Moscow physicist, believed that psychics have the ability to synchronize their subcellular molecular changes to generate gravitational fields to access and affect a target. I find it interesting that just in the past decade it has been discovered that magnetic particles exist in the human brain in small quantities.

Getting to the core of ESP is fundamentally challenging. Nevertheless, distinctions have been presented that allow us a peek into what give the brain the ability to perform unusual mental feats. We can look to the brains of savants for relevant comparison of heightened human perceptibility.

In her book *ESP Enigma: The Scientific Case for Psychic Phenomena*, neuroscientist and Harvard-trained psychiatrist Diane Hennacy Powell explains:

> *Autistic savants are a prime example of people who obtain information through heightened perception rather than the usual analytical channels...In addition to having the typical savant skills in mathematics, art, music, and memory, some savants have psychic abilities... Savant skills are usually enhanced right brain functions and savants' deficits are in the left brain abilities...In dreaming and autism there is a shift in dominance, so the limbic system and sensory cortices are more dominant...increased activity in the limbic system will increase the activity of the intuitive, creative right brain and inhibit the analytical, linear, and logic-based left brain...*

Not all people tune out background noise to the same degree. According to Dr. Powell, people who are open-minded, creative or intelligent score lower on tests of *latent inhibition*—the reduction of attention to stimuli. These people tune out less background information. In contrast, the more we use the analytical parts of our brains and go into situations with preconceptions, the more we increase our latent inhibition. Could that be why extremely analytical people have fewer psychic experiences?

Speaking of hemispheric asymmetry, I intuited myself that one possible area of the brain responsible for psychic functioning is the angular gyrus. It doesn't hurt to ponder so I looked it up. An online blog, *The Brain From Top to Bottom*, by the Canadian Institutes of Health Research, Institute of Neuroscience, explains it as follows:

> *Brain areas such as these, which perform high-level integration functions, are more heterogeneous than areas that perform primary functions. This greater heterogeneity might reflect greater sensitivity to environmental influences and greater plasticity (ability to adapt to them). The functional organization of language would even appear to vary within the same individual at various stages of his or her life!*

> *Together, the angular and supramarginal gyri constitute a multimodal associative area that receives auditory, visual, and somatosensory inputs. The neurons in this area are thus very well positioned to process the phonological and semantic aspect of language that enables us to identify and categorize objects.*

On a macroscopic anatomical level, folds and grooves in the brain vary greatly from individual to individual. There is interindividual variability. In his book, *The Power of Premonitions,* Dr. Larry Dossey explains that "brain function can vary dramatically in normal humans." His book carefully defines factors that make some individuals prone to premonition and he sympathizes that "some will try to shame you for experiencing it." According to Dr. Dossey these factors include absorption, belief in the transcendent, a sense of the unity of all life, compassion and empathy, intuition, comfort with chaos and disorder, external locus of control, meaning, interest and positivity, respect for the unconscious, personality type and common sense.

There is a deep area of the brain called the hippocampus, which is the driver of our autonomic nervous system and involved with our most primal memories and emotions. Dr. Dossey describes a study at Washington University in St. Louis involving fMRI (functional MRI) brain scans in normal subjects. "Memory processing centers in the brain are activated when individuals imagine potential future events. The discovery that the hippocampus is involved in visualizing the future may be important in understanding premonitions."

Most people allow their psychic sense to atrophy, never using it. Others bring it out and develop it into a highly tuned force or skill. Like all human abilities, some people will never excel at it, and some people will be exceptional.

> *Rebecca's talent is truly amazing. When I visited her, she told me things about my family and boyfriend that I thought were maybe a little bit off... but asking them later, they said that everything she said was one hundred percent true. There is absolutely no way she could be "cold-reading" these things; I didn't even know them myself! She knew that my sister has anger problems and is allergic to peanut butter, that my boyfriend used to stutter and that he loves puns and is a great artist, that mother had a painful relationship with her mother (something I was not aware of). Either Rebecca has had constant surveillance of my life for the past 30 years, or she has an incredible gift. I know what I believe!*
>
> —Claire

Dr. Dossey continues: "Might those individuals who have a gift for premonitions have a 'hippocampal advantage' that enables them to better see the future? My theory: perhaps there should be an ESP-IQ test.

I think it's significant that our western society has not grasped the benefits of meditation, because it has been shown to be a type of precursor to psychic experience. Dr. Powell says that meditation "synchronizes the activity of the two hemispheres such that the left brain is no longer dominant. EEGs of experienced meditators show more coherent, or lower-frequency, brain waves when they are meditating."

Those who disparage ESP often refer to it as "mind reading" cheapening it to an unworthy magician's trick. Well, not exactly. Instead, for these purposes, let's call it mind *feeling*. In other words, deep empathy. We vibrate in response to other frequencies.

Again, science has already validated this claim. Dr. Powell explains: "Vibration creates interconnectivity because of a physical phenomenon called resonance." Resonance, discovered in 1655 by a Dutch physicist, is the phenomenon in which one object influences another's vibration. Dr. Powell explains that *limbic resonance* is the ability of most mammals to become attuned to the inner states of others. "Resonance occurs at the subatomic level among members of the same species, since they share many of the same genes. Resonance would also occur to some degree across species, since animals all share many of the same genes."

Even that familiar saying "gut feeling" has a scientific basis. Elecrogastrogram (ECG) electrodes placed on the abdomen's skin can measure activity in the gut. Dr. Powell explains that "a more primitive 'brain,' or neural network, in the gut is thought to be involved in emotional responses, or 'gut reactions,' which can occur in the gut independent of the brain. The gut contains one hundred million neurons and is the only organ other than the brain with such a complex neural network." It's not just superstition.

Ulisse Di Corpo and Antonella Vannini Cox describe a real-life example of gut feeling at work. In an article in the Journal of the American Society of Psychical Research, they discuss a 1956 study by W. E. Cox on the use of commuter trains in the United States. "Cox discovered a lower presence of commuters on trains that had accidents. Comparing the number of passengers who boarded trains which had accidents with the number of passengers who boarded the same train, at the same time and day of previous weeks, Cox discovered that the number of passengers on trains that had accidents was significantly inferior to what would have been expected, and that this reduction could not be explained as a consequence of chance."

Despite the fact that the term "ESP" has been around since the 1950s, and despite all of the scientific investigations into the working of the brain and psychic abilities, we are still a society that acts as if it ESP were somehow a foreign gateway to some forbidden place. It's not. It is a commonly shared, natural experience. Scientists around the globe use it.

Jonas Salk said, "Intuition will tell the thinking mind where to look next."

There are two things that really stand in the way of my field becoming more widely appreciated. The first is the great divide between those who misuse the term psychic as a way to exploit others for entertainment value and those who seek to promote these abilities for the betterment of mankind. The second is the efforts of those who want to stymie understanding and achievement of true psychic powers, mostly because of preconceptions and fear.

Dr. Powell believes that as more scientists become aware of the evidence, "innovative corporations will increasingly pour resources into psi applications. There is no doubt that whoever develops psi-based practical applications will become the leaders of twenty-first-century high technology. The tide of industrial interest has already turned in Asia, and Europe is close behind. The United States lags the rest of the world in this regard."

And all of us know if you want to hear something with better perception you can turn off the lights or close your eyes so your ocular vision does not overload your brain—allowing you to focus solely on your sense of hearing. One particular sense can be deepened or extended by toning down unnecessary distractions. It's the same with clairvoyance. But the ultimate quest is to synthesize *all* of the senses, to envision the big picture and to see the whole world.

There is scientific evidence for remote viewing. Remote viewing entails a scientifically-based protocol of accessing details of a target which is distant or shielded. Physicist Russell Targ is a renowned laser physics pioneer. He co-founded the Stanford Research Institute's investigations into applications of psychic functioning in the 1970s for the CIA. At my last count he has written or co-written eight books on psychic abilities and remote viewing.

After thoroughly studying his books, I attended his workshop on remote viewing, ESP, precognition, intuitive diagnosis and distant healing, sponsored by the Rhine Research Center on the campus of Duke University in North Carolina. In a compelling, scientific presentation he explained his work.

Dr. Targ conducted remote viewing research and operations over a twenty-year period for the U.S. Army and Air Force Intelligence, the DIA, CIA, the U.S. Navy and NASA. Twenty million dollars was spent on the project. There were 23 mostly military viewers on this top secret program between 1972 and 1995 and they successfully assisted the government on numerous occasions, including in 1978 when viewers located a downed Soviet backfire bomber with code books on board when satellites were unable to locate it and in 1980 when viewers described the secret construction of a "Typhoon" Submarine, an imminent national security concern.

All through the presentation, I was on the edge of my seat, waiting until the big moment when Dr. Targ would give *us* his remote viewing test! He stood beside a cloaked object, and the crowd fell silent as he commanded: "I have a target that needs a description. Tell me about the surprising element that appears in your awareness. Write down any words that come bubbling up…" Though he was quiet, he seemed somewhat excited, awaiting our results.

I sketched a circular image or symbol, with jagged edges and I thought to myself, *like some kind of "astrological sign,"* like the zodiac that has all those symbols around it in clockwise formation. I picked up the descriptors *gold* and *metal* and drew a woman's face up in the corner, with long curly hair and a hat at the top and added a snake down in the corner.

When he uncloaked his object, we were presented with a golden metallic representation of "Shiva" framed within a jagged circular border. Though not an astrological sign it was of a similar tradition, one with which I was totally unfamiliar. (Shiva is a complicated Hindu deity with the iconographical features of a snake around his neck and a crescent moon flowing from his long, matted hair, who holds a trident, sits on a tiger skin and is believed to be at the core of the centrifugal force of the universe.) My mind related to it as close as it could. Although my sketch lacked the extra arms, it had many correlating features.

There are a large number of existing studies that connect remote viewing to psi. Here are two:

B.J. Dunne, R.G. Jahn, and R.D. Nelson, "Precognitive Remote Perception," *Princeton Engineering Anomalies Research Laboratory* (Report), August 1983:

> *In the most comprehensive laboratory examination of precognition, 227 formal experiments involving viewers asked to describe where one of the researchers would be hiding at a preselected later time. As Targ described in The Limitless Mind, "They discovered, much to their surprise, that the accuracy of the description was the same whether they viewer*

*had to look hours or days into the future. The sta-
tistical significance of the combined experiments departed from chance by a probability of 10-11, or one
in a hundred billion! Their findings are so strong
that it is hard to read about their work and not be
convinced of the reality of precognition, even though
we don't understand how it works.*

More of Targ's research can be studied in his book *Memoirs
of a Blind Biker*. As Targ says in *The Mind Race*, ""The greatest
favor that one scientist can do for another is to replicate his or her
work." J. Bisaha and B.J. Dunne published "Precognitive Remote
Viewing in the Chicago Area: A replication of the Stanford
Experiment, Research in Parapsychology, 1976 (Metuchen,
N.J.:Scarecrow:1977), pp.84-86. Dunne and Bisaha's paper was
the first replication of the SRI remote-viewing research. It showed
that high-quality remove viewing could be found somewhere
other than in our laboratories in California. Bisaha and Dunne
Conclude:

*The results of these two experiments provide further
evidence of the apparently widespread availability
of a perceptual/communication channel in which
time and distance appear to pose no barriers, and
which seems to become accessible when ordinary
modes of perception and communication become in-
operable. It further appears that this channel can be
"tuned into" by individuals with no extraordinary
psychic ability...it is our conclusion that precognitive remote perception techniques can acquire statistically significant amounts of compounded information about spatially and temporally remote target
locations, by means currently inexplicable by known
physical mechanisms.*

This is only a glimpse of available research. A theory of my own is that our minds may be evolving in synch with new types of threats to mankind. We share interlocking destinies.

Given that throughout history there seems to be infighting among scientists, we can't expect science journalism to be beating down a path in this direction. This stymies the dissemination of knowledge.

There is an energy highway that exists yet is transparent. It serves as an exchange of warnings and guidance and is what came to be known as our "intuitive senses." It's not a game; it's perfect and adequate for the body to have an extra set of senses from the here and now. This is a very important and fundamental human process going on. Our body will allow us this gift of knowledge which can lead to recovery, aid and protection where and when it matters. It's definitely not frivolous. Learn to use your intuition and watch yourself grow in the most delicate, artful, spiritual, soulful and compassionate way.

We are getting closer to a theory of universal consciousness, that all things are connected—all matter and minds. Let us, behaviorally elevate ourselves, constructively, resourcefully and consciously to be better people, to solve our problems, to be more in-touch with what is happening around us and to be safe.

✵ Afterword: Lessons of Inspiration

Do not wait for leaders; do it alone, person to person.

—Mother Teresa

I can tell the future, unconsciously, as easy as breathing. Please understand, this a big deal for me. I was once overwhelmed. But I still needed to offer this gift to the world. We all should seek to use these gifts, not to keep them contained.

It seems at times like no one understands or cares how immense this ability feels to me. Like everyone else, I needed understanding and resources in order to develop my gifts. I am lucky that I have begun to find them.

I face many struggles because I let this profession choose me. I'm a sensitive person. That's why I'm able to exercise my psychic abilities. I deal with a lot of nasty remarks and comments and it's hard not to take them personally. It is difficult to get respect.

As I said earlier, there are too many charlatans and no regulation in this profession, which hurts everyone. If there were licensing or certification, true psychics would welcome being tested to protect the consumer.

A client once advised against calling myself psychic, because it scares people, but instead a "guide," because that's what I am.

There is still religious fear despite the fact that many saints were purported to have has psychic experiences. Any God *I* can believe in would be a well-spring of love, information and vibration—and have some way for us to tap into these. Otherwise, what's the point?

We should never have to feel threatened. "You have a gift from God and it's precious," a client told me. The gift is not for me, it is for the people who listen to me. Please listen. We need to open our hearts to allow peace to come in and take over. I am becoming more acquainted not with God's word, but God's way. It can be found in little things and seeks to protect the innocent here on earth.

> *You got me back; re-motivated me...I've been waiting for that information for forty years. It really gave me some confidence. You helped me approach what's going on and start working on it. I can't thank you enough!*
>
> —Daniel

For part of my life I felt left out by the religious community, but now I realize that I belong to the shelter of God no matter what signage I use. And faith can open doors. I sense a tender grace around me. It's spiritual, there's no doubt about it. It's based in love and forgiveness and directs that compassion in this world is a necessity. All of us here have lessons to learn, through which together we can overcome any adversity.

There *are* messengers of the divine in this world, impelled to deliver messages and warnings that may save innocent lives. Yes, there is something greater than us working for good, when and where it can.

I know now that I'm not the only one to have taken this kind of journey. I hear time and time again people telling me they want their family to accept that they are having premonitions and pre-cognitive dreams, but their fear of rejection, from being told they sound crazy, makes them keep it to themselves.

My plea to the world: if you are in a position of power or authority, and someone comes to you with a message or information that might help you prevent something terrible from happening, don't push them away. It's urgent, and it doesn't hurt to listen. That's all they ask.

✦ Appendix I
Interviewing the Universe

We are Divine enough to ask and we are important enough to receive.

—Wayne Dyer

Seeking answers to questions of the spiritual components behind life, I went straight to the source in a way I singularly trust. To begin an automatic writing (flow of consciousness) session I angle my perception to a cool and somehow sensuous state, peacefully drifting, allowing my inner psyche to parlay the words I need.

I am making no attempt to influence anyone one way or the other. This is entirely original material; it is not formed from a compilation of my experience, imagination or other existing texts.

Can you give an overview of these contexts of spirituality?

Belief is a system. You can center your existence around yourself, or can reach out beyond, for what is alive yet passive. It is a personal choice. But, all in all, no one really understands who or what this is. There are many types of labels. It is very still. Its messages are conveyed to us by a hierarchy of what I call Angels. We, as humans, need help all the time. Problems must be solved.

There is too much hate within humans. Those who do not seek will, of course, never find. The answer is within you.

> *The family story I heard my grandmother Bee tell us one Christmas was that when my mom was little, she began exclaiming "I believe in Angels," and carried on about it.*
>
> *My grandmother told her, "We're Unitarian. You don't have to believe in angels but you can believe what you want."*
>
> *"Okay," she said. "I want to believe in Angels."*
>
> —Rebecca Bartlett

What is psychic ability?

Psychic ability is the threshold of our cognitive processing to obtain information beyond qualities exhibited by our local perceptive awareness or outside the realm of our more external physical senses.

It is a sense that lies at an underdeveloped region of our brain out of touch of any researcher yet connects us to multiple and parallel dimensions within and around our consciousness. It can be used or simply ignored. But there is a sense of knowing within all of us if we reach into deeper and deepest levels of our consciousness—or our soul's energy and reunite with them as needed to live a stronger more compassionate existence, we will experience peace and total awareness of our lives and the lives of those around us. This brings our existence into a fuller compatibility with Mother Nature enhancing all of our instincts that as human beings we obviously need to work harder at. It's the greatest power that comes from within and is ultimately very fulfilling and it does have a drive all its own and very creative energy.

"Abilities" are simply mental avenues leading to perception and qualities thereof including the assimilation of knowledge like a siphon inside our brain's right hemisphere. Intuition will bridge a gap from today and tomorrow, space and matter. It's indestructible. It has many corresponding parts. It's in the mitochondrial DNA; a regular part of our systems. It is not intrinsically divine in origin. It evolves within the corpus collosum. Brain waves change as this muscle flexes to gather intuitive material to constructively use. Chemistry is involved and cerebral spinal fluid. Bodily reactions are involved. It is systemic work that takes a high amount of the body's energy. It is extra cellular. It deals with gravitational fields. It has a kinetic appeal; anti-matter; self powered. Put your brains into it, not out of it. Let it do its thing and it can and will provide you with the most miraculous results, if awareness is what you are seeking.

What is the soul?

There is great debate over nature of consciousness and the existence of the soul. The soul is like a shield delivering inspiration and messages to us throughout our life. The soul can indeed be measured. It does vibrate at a different pitch. Someone who is about to die has a soul that has shifted and is no longer so strongly tethered to the bodies' organs. It encompasses our being. It's three dimensional. It can grow. It is normally what we would associate with the color light blue. It has a healing ability and all knowingness. It is also our body's internal alarm letting us know when something isn't right, guiding us at times. It does indeed have personality, individual to us each. It plays hard to get. It's locked in our consciousness. It plays a part in manufacturing our reality. It can shield us from negativity if we trust it, and actually it's very dense like a vapor or a cloud. It shifts and can have its own projection. It is truly the nature or the greater part of the nature of our individual psyches.

It is our spirit energy…a storehouse…the ethereal composite of our elemental makeup. It is the psychic template of our being, our spiritual manifestation - our astral component.

Can a soul communicate through signals?

Yes, it can convey information it wants you to know. It can manipulate electrostatic frequencies—our earth energies, dream implantation, medium telepathy, and very rarely, re-forming energy to appear to us.

Can the soul be re-born into another human body?

Yes, in cases of re-schooling and punishment.

Does the soul ever leave the body before death?

It is rare and may occur in cases of trauma. In an altered state of consciousness and reality the body will separate.

When you die does your soul go on living?

Not all pass through. Some get trapped and cannot move out of this plane of existence. It is not as easy as it seems.

What is past-life regression?

Keys to our consciousness, buried memories, lost lives. There is a history there that is profound and involves all genders. Through deep hypnosis we can recall past lives and remove obstacles in present time, some pain, and re-live the past. Sometimes in dreams we go back to a past of all our past lives. Karma does play a big part in reincarnation chains.

What is the aura?

An aura is an energy trail. It is our soul's fingerprint. All the information is there.

Can people heal themselves?

Yes. The body's chemistry is built to heal in accordance with our needs and direction of our inner spirit, drive, or intention. Remember, breath is life. Use the energy around you and take cues from your environment to cure.

What are angels?

Different angels have different duties. They are all to serve and protect, not create. They have special powers. They cannot be seen under most circumstances. They are heard more easily. They come to comfort us, be our guidance, our soul's caretaker. They are essentially beings of light. One cannot control them with earthly desires and wishes. They are compassionate friends. Some people on earth are Angels sent to help humanity. You never can tell.

Are there spirit guides that previously lived on earth that now guide us?

This is sort of correct. They can be thought of as our inner voice and help us get connected with the other side. They are our predecessors. They are also a spiritual liaison to the afterworld. They are impartial and free of bias. They guide us, but they don't actually work to protect us. They can help us heal.

How can we contact spirit guides?

It is very difficult to get a spirit guide.

There are no standard modes or verses for communication. Patience, perception, trial and error garner and solicit contact with other dimensions of higher power than we possess. You can't just snap your fingers. It may take time, energy and perseverance. No two are the same. Also, there is not necessarily a permanent guide for you. They come and they go as needed. They do not play up to your whims and commands or demands. They are full of grace and temperance.

It takes a great deal of work and practicing to contact spirit guides. In essence you are becoming a medium—they are on another dimension than ours.

The differentiation between their messaging and our subconscious takes time to develop for this higher sense and to tune into their subtle energy.

We are all psychic; it's just a matter of degree. You don't just have one spirit guide; you could be consoled by three at one time. There are beings on other planes that want to help us, who want to work with us to be happy and improve ourselves.

If everybody could pick this up easily no one would need to see a professional psychic. Initially you will defeat yourself because you have so many doubts. It will come to you eventually. They won't give us fame. Won't give us fortune, but they will impart wisdom. Consider them a circle of friends.

What is Heaven?

Heaven is a different dimension than that we are accustomed to. It is a school for soul's perfection and cleansing. It is an exit point from our time to a plane of higher existence—or energy.

Explain the passageways to the afterlife.

The direction the soul moves is from West to East. North is negative—devoid of light. "Not to fear, your angel is near."

Your soul leaves through your heart. There is a golden chord that is cut. You drift now toward a higher, ethereal consciousness very quickly. You become entwined with the joy that envelops you. Your soul is now free of its corporeal body.

You are born into a new route, or re-routed. If you are allowed to gain entry you come to a staging place for re-birth.

Is there really a bright light?

There is an ethereal, translucent light of joy and ecstasy beyond comprehension or description.

Is it true that once we're over there we get to conjure up anything we want?

You get peace. Anything you want? How material! Inappropriate. You receive forgiveness, a second chance, a realization. Love, pure Love. Wholeness and oneness with the world. No misery and you won't need all those trappings of the material world.

You still don't own yourself. You don't do anything you want. Your soul is on a growing journey to evolve. It is not like winning the lottery or Disneyland without limits. It's like a school.

You will receive what you deserve based on the life you led. You will experience all the pain you made others feel. It cuts to the bone.

Bad people must be held in isolation for a number of days. There is punishment. They learn and they move on. They must make up their misdeeds before they can pass on to the next realm. This is the Penalties phase.

Some do refuse to leave. They need time. You can't help them.

When you have crossed over how are you restored?

You are complete. But you are ethereal, not physical, so

therefore there would be no physical pain to be experienced once you reach this phase.

Who is waiting for you on the other side?

Three angels, a spiritual guide or guides, and the God Source, which can be defined as light, pure healing love energy.

You see the relatives passing along through the spherical tunnel/gateway toward the heaven realm to ease you, but they don't just stand there for you waiting.

Your past will play out like a movie reel. You are renewed.

If you take your own life will you be punished for eternity?

This is false. Forgiveness rules. Life is flexible. No end anyhow to life. Not so fatalistic. Next comes a review.

Do the dead have a concept of time?

Time is an energy that just gets used up or transferred to something else – some other force or form. It is light they operate on, and some plasma residue. They don't have time. It is an endless expanse and a journey toward improvement.

Can the departed come to you in a dream?

Yes, because it's easier for them to connect with you then.

How do our pets fit into the mix?

Cats, dogs and horses *are* higher powers. They are not "creatures" that are disposable. They are here to help and guide people, be our companions, our eyes and ears. For example, look at their ability to love unconditionally which surpasses our own. They do supply messages, emotional support, ease our pain. No two are the same. They have excellent memories. They would give their lives to keep us safe. They are friends and guardians to us.

Do animals have sixth sense?

Sure. And we were once more like them also. Until we became more sheltered and industrialized, as that replaced our other senses. Also they have an internal antenna and telescope into time that we lack. They are "bred" for these certain instincts beyond our own. Treating a pet well is very important.

Can animals pick up on spirits?

Their vision cuts through all dimensions; yes.

What is the Bible?

A plan for reconstructing peace on our planet and a source of inspiration. A code for life (everything's there). The first code has been broken. There are additional codes—three— remaining.

It's where to start to look for inspiration. Don't worship the bible; inherit a more significant message from its pages. Use it as a stepping stone. The bible is not meant for hatred or antipathy to divide. It is a certain resource, but to be taken with a grain of salt. It means the smallest can be the mightiest, and that justice will be delivered based upon our deeds. That we are never alone, really.

Here is one final theme, combining inspiration and my own thoughts.

How is the mind separate from the brain?

The mind is a dynamic entity which is able to change, make measured changes in an environment and affect things with some invisible force of nature.

First you must try to understand, where do thoughts arrive from? Do they arrive from the brain or are they stimulated by something separate? And if these thoughts have energy, is that energy caused by some form of neuron processing within the brain or just the power of desire itself?

And what is the faculty taking over when we dream, especially when an awareness comes into our dreams of events of the future? It's fascinating that not only can we visualize these things, but remember them upon waking. That means we must fully not be asleep if we actually remember what happened. The dream has left such an impression upon our souls.

Should we first ask what the brain is because we don't have the answer to that, and then follow up with what is time because nobody seems to have correct models that they can agree upon. What exactly is a human feeling? You know I think sometimes a feeling is so powerful it never dies. It spans somewhere throughout time. And how does the heart enter all of this and what is more powerful—the heart, the mind, the soul?

So what exactly is consciousness? Is consciousness the operating system of the mind or is consciousness actually the energy of time? Maybe we are not just bodies but we are also time—united forces in a very entangled universe. It's true, though, if there are photons and light is an energy, and there are photons in our body then we would obviously resonate with light and interact innately with constant fields as such.

The mind is the harbor of our awareness and a telepathic portal. The mind has kinetic energy properties, telekinetic energy properties, the ability to bilocate, trilocate, and reverse order in the field of physics—a principle of quantum dynamics. It is able to work outside of our conscious awareness throughout time— physical of metered time, legered time. It is abstract, ethereal, intimate in the order of the universe, behaves like a muscle, takes its fuel like an engine, power can be increased with the focused concentration joined by other minds. Again, operates outside of time, really does what is best for us, tells us what is best for us, can be very directing of intentions to us. It cannot be quantified. It feels, it endures, it expands, it unites, is ever present, belongs to us, holds the key that goes into the lock of all of our perceptions. Consciousness is our state of mind.

To begin with, consciousness is the root of our awareness. It is our own tuning fork. We know we can change it at will or through the suggestion of another. So it is quite malleable. It doesn't necessarily have to do with a mental state, has more to do with a spacial state in a sense of, let's say manufacturing time that we want to see things or to be places, aware of things. It's completely fragile and can be manipulated to induce states of healing or higher energy changes. It circumvents our brains, exists outside and inside our minds, or bodies, it is a puzzle, it is a state of wakefulness, its energy is strongest nearest our solar plexus. It can't justly be described in terms that we have available to us today. Sometimes it seems to make up its own mind what it wants to do. It has certain levels, or energy fluctuations, from dull to high. People excite or dispel neural, neuron activity in our brains, but to a certain degree it is very omnipotent.

Okay, so call it a psychic power house, in it exists the origin of thought, the accumulation of our memories, brain storage—like extra disc space, really. So it's multilayer, complex, driven from within and without, is sensitive, yet feels no pain, and again shifts under signals throughout time if we are observant enough to these small, subtle mental cues. It's sort of like a double brain to us, on a type of holographic scale.

🐾 Appendix II
How to Recognize a True Psychic

Psychics get a bad rap in the minds of many people. Like any profession, there are crooks and cheats. But there are also authentic psychics whose aim is to help mankind and whose motive is love.

How can you know who's real and who's not? Debunking all of us is unjust. The gold standard is still word-of-mouth. That won't help you if you haven't had your ear to the ground, so please read this chapter. Just for comparison, I want to share with you a few first-hand accounts I've heard from my clients. A woman came in to see me, and in the process of her reading she shared that she had seen every type of intuitive provider from here to the moon.

One of them told her there was "a hole in her aura that became a portal to a new dimension." This, she said, was the actual source of pain in her side and the noises in her house she needed help with. This seems highly implausible, yet these are the kinds of whacko things out there, everywhere, and the cause of great frustration on my part to be seen in a positive light.

To begin with, an authentic psychic will tell you to reveal nothing about yourself before the reading. Some fraudulent psychics use scripted generalities rather than honing in on you. At the same time, they will try to glean information from you rather than give it.

The expectation is on me to provide proof of my abilities. My directive is not merely to give you the name of your spirit guide.

Look at the psychic's appearance and office. Is it calming or scary? Dark or light? Are there gimmicks and snake-oil products they want you to purchase? Examples of snake oil products are stop smoking and weight loss aids.

Watch out for any brand of reader who tells you up front that you have "bad" energy or are cursed. They will try to sell you services or potions that will "take the curse away." Part of their trick is to ask for your money to take the supposed curse off of it. These are extreme cases, of course.

One client told me she saw someone who wanted her to spend $300 for a $2 pink quartz crystal that would heal her. I don't sell things; the soul is not a commodity, but information is, and this is the age of information. A young student who hailed from the Ukraine called me to assess whether her lover would come back after she confronted him over his unwillingness to work and he angrily moved out. I gave her all the information I could.

But, when it comes to unrequited love many people get desperate. She called later on down the road in her thick accent to tell me that she had found a woman through an ad in the newspaper and paid her $1,000 to perform a love spell on her ex-boyfriend. Evidently, the woman's spell didn't work. Neither the spell nor all the candles she was told to light had the desired effect on her love interest.

It is wise to look for a psychic who gives some kind of description in specific terms of what she does or doesn't do and how she works. This is a sign of being ethical and sensitive to the needs of one's clientele. Learn if they have a guarantee. If they can't read you, you shouldn't pay.

I was taken aback when a reputable psychic's website said she covered health (in one small, non-descriptive sentence), but when I asked a health question she replied: "I'm really not good at health stuff." Take some time to look for these factors and it will pay off.

> *Your gift is very valuable! I can only imagine what you must have gone through to get there and I commend you for it. Previously I had a reading from someone very negative who overcharged for her time—half of which she wasted on speaking about esoteric nonsense... You have changed my life...now I'm on my way to heal! Thank you.*
>
> —J.A.

Throughout the years that I've been in business a number of women have come to me in tears after seeing a palm reader who advised them that their husbands were going to die. (One did not even have a husband.) What I do is life-*affirming*.

One of the very few readings I've ever received was offered to me in exchange for my reading her. She was a professional making triple what I do, but her reading really depressed me.

At the outset she began muttering "North, South, West..." She was using cards and I was left out of the loop. She offered no actual psychic impressions, just intuition that was sparse at best, and nothing of any value to me. I felt completely drained at the end, and in the whole half hour I was only allowed to ask three questions after which I waited and waited as she shuffled the cards to come up with an "answer." I felt so sorry for her clients.

This work is something intangible, involving a unique dynamic of the human condition. Bear in mind a reading is not put to use only for that hour, but hopefully guides one for years to come.

It's difficult to determine the right price for the services. There are definitely varying degrees of skill. Common sense advice is that the price should be relative to the strength of the gifts, their value, and the experience and track record being offered. A psychic can charge anything her clients will accept, like an artist or hair dresser. Some psychics are underpaid and some are overpaid.

The price should not be exorbitant. A reasonable fee for an excellent, experienced psychic is two hundred dollars an hour in most areas of the country. In the most expensive cities, it could be more.

Sometimes it's just based on popularity. I believed a famous psychic was legit after seeing her television spots and was kind of mesmerized. Then one day I happened to watch one of her YouTube posts and could sense she was not actually "connecting." She was faking it. She put on such a convincing show for others that I think she got to a point that she even convinced herself. This is a case where sometimes achieving fame is more indicative of entrepreneurial skills than genuine abilities. I next went to her website and found a red flag. There she warned clients she is the *only* psychic they should *ever* see. No one person is the best or holds all the answers. This was made apparent in her case on down the road.

There are some people who only seek out the services of a psychic as entertainment at a party. I steer away from parties. I could be put in a room with a lot of "distractors" (photos, books, etc...) vying for my attention. It's not conducive to how I need to work; I am not a side show.

In closing, I think psychics should be certified or licensed as authentic. It would give a needed professionalism to the occupation as well as protect the consumer. I brought up this issue in person with Sally Rhine Feather, Ph.D., a researcher with the Rhine

Research Center. She replied that one group in particular is now providing testing and certification for mediums. That's progress!

So, we've come a long way so far. Still there are many authentic psychics who do not work in the field because it is so hard to make a living. One can make money as a crook, unfortunately, and there are many who do! If you find a true psychic who makes you feel better, not worse, you have a gem—hang onto them.

❀ About the Author

Rebecca Bartlett has practiced her psychic abilities for twenty five years. She has a successful professional integrative psychic business of personal and telephone readings with clients throughout the United States. She has published articles in an Indianapolis magazine and presented on radio shows. She studied at Indiana University and in Greece. She resides outside of Nashville, in Bean Blossom, Indiana.